Early
Quaker Records
of
Southeast Virginia

Martha A. Putnam

HERITAGE BOOKS
2020

HERITAGE BOOKS

AN IMPRINT OF HERITAGE BOOKS, INC.

Books, CDs, and more—Worldwide

For our listing of thousands of titles see our website
at
www.HeritageBooks.com

Published 2020 by
HERITAGE BOOKS, INC.
Publishing Division
5810 Ruatan Street
Berwyn Heights, Md. 20740

International Standard Book Number
Paperbound: 978-1-58549-332-6

Table of Contents

INTRODUCTION

For a complete description of early Quakerism in Virginia see Phebe R. Jacobsen, *Quaker Records in Maryland*, and William Wade Hinshaw, *Encyclopedia of American Quaker Genealogy*.

Chuckatuck Meeting was formed in Nansemond County around 1673 and soon thereafter a meeting at Pagan Creek in Isle of Wight County. By 1767 the name of Chuckatuck Monthly Meeting had been replaced as Western Branch Monthly Meeting.

Blackwater (later called Surry) Monthly Meeting was formed by 1765 when the men's minutes begin. At that time this monthly meeting encompassed the counties of Surry, Sussex, Prince George and Dinwiddie.

If Pagan Creek ever was a monthly meeting it ceased to function as such by 1763. In 1792, Pagan Creek Meeting was discontinued and joined to Blackwater Monthly Meeting.

A sense of the membership of Blackwater [Surry] and Western Branch [Chuckatuck] can be judged by the lists on pages 12-13 and 52-53 where I show copies of the names of male members of the Society, by county, which were listed in order to be exempted from militia duty in 1767. The counties listed for Blackwater were Prince George, Sussex, Southampton, Isle of Wight, Dinwiddie, and Surry. At the same time the list for Western Branch Monthly Meeting included the names of male members from the counties of Nansemond, Norfolk (2 names), Isle of Wight and Southampton.

Abbreviations:

b. - born

dau. - daughter

d. - died

dec. - deceased

Phrases:

certificate - a letter recognizing the person or persons as upstanding members of the society, with their affairs in order and clear of marriage engagements (when indicated)

disorderly marriage - a marriage outside the society

hireling priest - a paid minister of some other denomination

sufferings - in most cases a poll tax or other payment to support the Anglican Church

to marry - announced their intentions to marry

Martha A. Putnam
Portsmouth, VA
1996

BLACKWATER MONTHLY MEETING

1760-1800

Births

Children of John Andrews and Sarah his second wife: Joseph b. 18/12/1786; Robert b. 15/2/1789; Martha b. 18/6/1791; Elizabeth b. 23/7/1793; John b. 2/4/179?. Jane (daughter of John Andrews and Jane his first wife) b. 23/6/1783, d. 27/10/1783. Jane Andrews (first wife of John Andrews) d. 23/6/1783.

Children of Joseph Butler and Miriam his wife of Dinwiddie County: Sarah b. 7/1/1769; William b. 6/4/1770; Margrat b. 30/12/1771; Robert Hunnicutt b. 19/8/1773; Micajah, b. 5/3/177-; Samuel, b. 9/6/1779; Edward, b. 3/3/1779; Martha, b. 26/11/1781.

Children of Joseph Butler of Dinwiddie County and Ann his wife: Elizabeth Butler b. 16/5/1769; James b. 11/6/1771; Tillman b. 6/10/1772; Martha b. 30/11/1773

Children of James Butler and Priscilla his wife of Dinwiddie County: Robert b. 23/9/1769; James b. 16/6/1771; Mary b. 30/9/1772; Tabitha, b. 24/2/1774; Jonathan, b. 3/10/1775; Sarah, b. 3/4/--; Ann, b. 28/9/1779; Elizabeth, b. 4/1/1782.

Children of Stephen Butler and Elizabeth his wife of Dinwiddie County: Hulda b. 13/10/1776; Elizabeth (Stephen Butler's wife) d. 13/2/1777.

Children of Joseph Butler and Priscilla his wife: Penninah b. 28/3/1777; Mary and Nancy, b. 20/7/1779; Lazarus, b. 15/3/1782.

Children of Elijah Bailey and Lucy his wife of Sussex County: William b. 6/7/1756; Sarah b. 29/12/1757; Patience b. 18/11/1759; Faith b. 5/8/1763.

Children of James Binford and Elizabeth his wife of Prince George County: Guli Elma b. 10/8/1774; Mary b. 18/8/1776.

Children of James Brock and Sara his wife: Burwell b. 31/8/1773; Martha b. 7/1/1775; Pharaby b. 27/6/1776.

Children of Edmond Bailey and Elizabeth his wife: Jesse, b. 2/2/1764; Mathew, 18/1/1767; James, b. 8/11/1768; Ann, b. 25/1/1771; Samuel, b. 5/6/1773; Micajah, b. 17/7/1775; Stephen, b. 15/11/1777.

Child of John and Elizabeth Butlar of Dinwiddie Co.: Lydia, b. 1/9/1778.

Children of Chappel and Martha Binford of Prince George Co.: Samuel, b., 20/3/1776; Lemuel, b. 6/10/1778; Robert, b. 28/5/1780; Peter, b. 16/1/1783; Chappell, b. 25/12/1785, d. 23/9/1794; Jane, b. 27/2/1788; Martha, b. 29/7/1790; Ann, b. 7/6/1793; Elizabeth, b. 30/10/1798.

Rachel Bailey, dau. of William and Rebecca Bailey of Sussex Co., b. 25/1/1780.

William Butlar, son of Stephen and Mary Butlar of Dinwiddie Co., b. 28/11/1779.

Children of Joseph and Mary Bailey of Sussex Co.: Miriam, b. 17 April 1756; Abigail, b. 25/1/1758; Joseph, b. 16/10/1761; Mary, b. 19/9/1764; John, b. 1/5/1766; Zachariah, b. 23/9/1775.

Children of Edmond Bailey and Elizabeth his wife: Jesse, b. 2/2/1764; Mathew, b. 18/1/1767; James, b. 8/11/1768; Ann, b. 25/1/1771; Samuel, b. 5/6/1773; Micajah, b. 17/7/1775; Stephen, b. 15/11/1777.

Peter Binford of Prince George Co., d. 24/1/1782; bur. 26th of same, age about 81 years.

Rebeckah Binford d. 2/2/1782; bur. 4th of same, age about 70 years.

Children of Abidan and Sarah Bailey: Rebeckah, b. 2/2/1774; David, b. 12/1/1776; Daniel, b. 31/12/1777; Josiah, b. 31/1/1780; Michal (dau.), b. 20/8/1782; Martha Bailey, b. 24/10/1784. Sarah Bailey, wife of Abidan, d. 30/1/1787.

Children of John and Martha Butler: Copeland, b. 18/4/1779; Josiah, b. 30/7/1781.

Joseph Butler, Senr., d. 17/1/1780, bur. 19th of same. Mary Butler, dau. of same dec. Joseph Butler and Ann his wife, d. 11/12/1781; bur. 13th of same.

Susanna Bailey, 2nd dau. of William and Rebeckah Bailey his wife, b. 10/2/1782.

James Stanton Butler, son of Stephen and Mary Butler, b. 31/7/1782.

Children of Joshua and Patience Bailey, Delitha b. 18/8/1775; Exam, b. 18/11/1777; Peninah, b. 15/3/1780; Lazerus, b. 20/11/1782.

Children of James and Sarah Brock his wife: Michal (dau.), b. 17/7/1781; d. 17/6/1782; Abigail, b. 15/3/1782.

Jonathan Butler, 1st son of John and Elizabeth Butler his wife, b. 8/3/1783.

Judith Bailey, 3rd dau. of William Bailey and Rebeckah his wife, b. 17/12/1783.

Children of Joshua Bailey and Patience his wife: Peterson, b. 15/4/1780, d. 25/8/1780; Gulie (dau.), b. 21/9/1783.

Benjamin Bailey, Senr., d. 24/11/1784.

Rhoda, dau. of James Brock and Sarah his wife, b. 4/7/1786.

Lucy, 4th dau. of William Bailey and Rebeckah his wife, b. 19/2/1784.

Elizabeth Butler, wife of John Butler, d. 8/9/1785.

Stephen, son of Stephen Butler and Mary his wife, b. 20/1/1786.

Ann Butler d. 20/5/1786.

Simon Butler, son of Joseph and the above Ann Butler, d. 22/7/1786.
Martha Butler, dau. of Joseph Butler and Miriam his wife, d. 29/5/1786.
Aquila Binford, 1st son of Peter Binford and Martha his wife, b. 9/1/1784.
Mary Binford, 1st dau. of the above Peter and Martha Binford, b. 17/5/1786.
Lucy Bailey, wife of Elijah Bailey, an Elder and member of Blackwater Meeting, d. 6/5/1786.
Joseph Butler, son of Joseph Butler and Miriam his wife, b. 19/11/1787, d. 14/4/1830.
Ann, dau. of Joshua Bailey and Patience his wife, b. 10/6/1786.
Bethany, 5th dau. of William Bailey and Rebecah his wife, b. 6/4/1788.
Children of James Binford and Elizabeth his wife: Gule Elma, d. 22/1/1782; Mary, b. 18/8/1776; Sarah, b. 19/12/1778; Rebeckah, b. 30/12/1780; Guli (dau.), b. 16/1/1783, d. 22/1/1782; Jonathan, b. 14/6/1785. Elizabeth, wife of said James Bindford, d. 11/11/1785.
Henry Butler, son of Joseph and Ann Butlar of Dinwiddie Co., d. 18/11/1788.
Burwell, son of James Brock and Sarah his wife, d. 19/10/1788.
Tilmon, son of Joseph Butler and his wife, d. 28/5/1789.
Jonthan, son of Steph Butler and Mary his wife, b. 29/4/1789.
Elizabeth, wife of Edmon Bailey, d. 30/10/1789/
Children of Peter Binford and Martha his wife: Peter, b. 18/10/1787, d. 31/8/1796; Martha, b. 8/12/1789. Martha wife of said Peter Binford, d. 24/12/1789.
Rebeckah, 6th dau. of William Bailey and Rebeckah his wife, b. 12/4/1790.
Joseph Butler, son of Joseph Butler and Miriam his wife, b. 19/11/1787, d. 14/4/1830.
Ann, dau. of Joshua Bailey and Patience, b. 10/6/1786.
Bethany, 5th dau. of William Bailey and Rebeccah his wife, b. 6/4/1788.
Benjamin, 1st son of Aquilla Binford and Mary his wife, b. 21/1/1791.
Children of James Butler and Priscilla his wife: Edward, b. 20/11/1783; Robert, b. 1/6/1787; Martha, b. 5/4/1790.
Margret Whitfield, dau. of Abidan Bailey and Mourning his 2nd wife, b. 16/12/1790.
James Butler, an Elder, and member of Gravely Run Meeting, d. 18/11/1791, in his 88th year.
Children of Joshua Bailey and Patience his wife: Ann, b. 10/6/1786; Edna, b. 26/8/1788; Mariah, b. 21/2/1790.
Wyatt, 1st son of William Bailey and Rebecca his wife, b. 13/5/1792.
Jane, 2nd wife of Elijah Bailey, d. 15/12/1792, she being a minister and member of Blackwater Meeting.

Elizabeth, dau. of Abadan Bailey and Mourning his wife, b. 15/12/1792.

Agness, 1st dau. of Aquilla Binford his wife, b. 8/4/1793.

Mourning, 2nd wife of Abidan Bailey, d. 18/9/1793.

James, son of Peter Binford and Martha his 2nd wife, b. 22/12/1793.

David, son of Stephen Butler and wife Mary, b. 13/4/1794, d. 19/7/1795.

Priscilla, dau. of William Bailey and Rebeckah his wife, b. 25/5/1794; d. 7/3/1795.

Robert, son of Joseph, deceased son of James Butler, d. 13/8/1794.

Samuel Bailey, an Elder and member of Blackwater Meeting, d. 27/6/1796.

Barak, son of William Bailey and Rebeckah his wife, b. 27/3/1796.

Children of Jesse Bailey and Pharaba his wife: Henry, b. 1/9/1793; Edmund, b. 2/10/1795; Abigal, b. 27/3/1798; Uriah, b. 27/11/1800.

Cirly, 2nd wife of John Butler, d. 25/8/1795.

John, son of Peter Binford and Martha his wife 2nd wife, b. 6/3/1795; Michal, dau. of above Peter Binford and Martha, b. 10/3/1797.

James, son of Daniel Butler and his wife Sarah, b. 17/12/1796; Mary, b. 12/8/1798.

Michal, dau. of William Bailey and Rebeckah, b. 27/1/1798.

Ann, dau. of Edmund Bailey and Elizabeth his wife, d. 8/7/1798.

Jonathan, 2nd son of Aquilla Binford and Mary his wife, b. 7/9/1798.

Children of Samuel Butler and Ursly his wife: Mourning, b. 9/8/1791; Nathan, b. 27/8/1793; Lucy, b. 26/10/1795; Lydia, b. 18/10/1797; Tabitha, b. 16/8/1799.

David, son of William Butler and Mary his wife, b. 27/7/1798.

Joseph Bailey, Elder and member of Seacock Meeting, d. 9/2/1802.

Elijah Bailey, an Elder and member of Seacock Meeting, d. 27/11/1800 in his 73rd year.

Permelia Bailey, dau. of Wm. and Rebecah his wife, b. 4/2/1801

Children of Benjamin Chappel and Agness his wife: Elizabeth, b. 13/9/1755; Thomas, b. 22/1/1758; John, b. 18/6/1760; Benjamin, b. 8/8/1763; Mary, b. 23/2/1766; Agness, b. 13/10/1768. Benjamin Chappell d. 11/3/1769, age about 45 years.

Children of Josiah and Lydia Cook: Priscilla b. 29/3/1782; Joel b. 19/6/1783; Betty b. 17/2/1785; John b. 25/9/1786.

Children of John and Judith Crew: Sarah Ladd b. 13/2/1785; Anne b. 8/2/1787; Joshua (2nd son) b. 1/3/1789; John Ellison b. 28/1/1791

Joshua Crew (son of John and Judith Crew of Mecklinburg) d. 13/8/1787.

Agness Chappell d. 6/7/1793, about 63 years old.

Children of Thomas and Jane Chappell: Mariah b. 17/5/1793.

Thomas Chappell d. 13/8/1793.

John Chappell d. 28/6/1796.
Children of Simmons and Mary Fowler: Martha b. 28/8/1765.
Elizabeth Fowler d. 7/8/1786.
Paul (son of Elizabeth Fowler) d. 11/5/1789.
Children of Wythe and Sarah Hunnicutt of Surry County: Sarah,
  30/3/1730; Glaister, b. 27/2/1732; Mary b. 3/9/1735 d. 7th month 1739;
  Robert b. 11/4/1737 d. 7th month 1739; Ruth b. 11/6/1740; Robert and
  Sarah (twins) b. 19/12/1742; Wythe, b. 11/12/1745.
Children of Wythe and Anna Hunnicutt of Prince George County: Lemuel
  b. 12/5/1770 d. 12/12/1775; Mary (1st daughter) b. 7/12/1772; Wythe
  b. 18/9/1775; Ann b. 26/11/1777; Lemuel (3rd son) b. 14/12/1779;
  Samuel (4th son) b. 3/1/1783; Anselm (5th son) b. 3/1/1787 d. 2/5/1788.
Glaister Hunnicutt d. 13/4/1781.
Josiah Hargrave d. 5/9/1778.
Children of Glaister and Jane Hunnicutt: Thomas Pleasant b. 24/8/1757
  d. 10/3/1758; Mary b. 5/1/1760; Sarah b. 14/7/1761; Pleasant (2nd son)
  b. 24/7/1768; Glaister b. 11/3/1766; Jane b. 31/12/1769.

--------------------P.G. County --------------------

Children of John and Mary Hunnicutt: Elizabeth b. 8/4/1763; Edward b.
  26/7/1764; Ephraim b. 21/10/1766; Ruth b. 13/1/1769.
Children of Robert and Ann Hunnicutt of Prince George County: Mary b.
  19/9/1755; Martha b. 24/9/175?; Jane 18/3/1759 d. 2/11/1759; Jane b.
  2/2/1761; Peter b. 11/5/1763 d. 18/5/1763; Elizabeth b. 18/6/1764;
  Sarah b. 5/11/1766 d. 23/11/1766; Thomas b. 22/5/1769.
Children of William and Mary Hunnicutt of Prince George County: Sarah
  b. 10/7/1763; Ann 21/5/1765; Mary 16/3/1767; James b. 30/1/1769;
  William b. 15/11/1770; Peter b. 13/3/1772 d. 2/7/1775.
Children of John and Mary Hunnicutt of Prince George County: Daniel
  (3rd son) b. 11/5/1771; Mark (4th son) b. 17/1/1774; Robert and Sarah
  b. 31/10/1776.
Children of William (son of Robert Hunnicutt) and Mary Hunnicutt; Jesse
  b. 15/7/1769; Susanna b. 8/4/1771 d. 4/1/1777.
Mary Hunnicutt (wife of the above William) d. 18/6/1775.
Children of William (son of Peter Hunnicutt) and Mary Hunnicutt of
  Dinwiddie County; John b. 9/2/1774 d. 3/7/1775; Martha (4th daughter)
  b. 6/6/1776; Elizabeth (5th daughter) b. 19/3/1778.
Children of Thomas and Miriam Hunnicutt of Prince George County:
  Sarah b. 30/10/1778; Mary 31/1/1780.
Children of William and Mary: Tabitha (6th daughter) b. 3/9/1780; Robert

(4th son) b. 15/9/1782.

Martha Hunnicutt (daughter of William and Mary Hunnicutt of Dinwiddie) d. 10/5/1785.

Children of Matthew and Mary Harris: Sarah b. 17/11/1775; Michal (2nd daughter) b. 7/1/1783.

Children of Thomas and Mirian Hunnicutt: Deborah (4th daughter) b. 23/10/1785.

Ann Hunnicutt (wife of Robert Hunnicutt and Elder and member of Burleigh Meeting) d. 8/11/1788.

Children of Matthew and Mary Harris: John and Samuel b. 4/2/1790

Children of Jesse and Susanna Hargrave: Hamlin b. 11/6/1773; Martha 14/11/1776; George b. 27/12/1776; Joseph b. 25/4/1779; Robert b. 21/8/1781; Benjamin b. 5/7/1784; John b. 21/4/1787; Jesse b. 30/12/1789.

Children of Charles and Martha Hamlin: Stephen b. 7/12/1781; Nancy b. 20/10/1783; William b. 10/11/1790.

Children of Clement and Mary Hicks: Laban b. 30/10/1789; James b. 29/1/1791.

Children of Richard and Ann Hargrave: Mary b. 5/8/1790.

Robert Hunnicutt (son of Peter, an Elder and member of Burleigh Meeting) d. 28/4/1795.

Children of Wythe and Ann Hunnicutt: John Pearson (6th son) b. 16/5/1791.

Children of John and Mary Hunnicutt: Robert and Martha b. 25/12/1779 (2nd pair of twins); Mary (5th daughter) b. 10/12/1782.

Elizabeth Hunnicutt (daughter of John and Mary Hunnicutt) d. 26/3/1793.

Children of Thomas and Mary Hunnicutt: James b. 12/9/1793.

Mary Hunnicutt, wife of Thomas Hunnicutt d. 1/11/1793.

Children of John and Margaret Havenridge: James b. 27/3/1794.

Children of Richard and Ann Hargrave: Elizabeth (2nd daughter) b. 2/10/1792; Matthew Jones b. 27/11/1794. Ann Hargrave (wife of Richard Hargrave) d. 24/2/1795.

Children of Thomas and Meriam Hunnicutt: Thomas b. 11/9/1794.

Children of James and Delitha Hunnicutt: Joshua Bailey b. 23/1/1797.

Susanna Hollowell (wife of William Hollowell of Isle of Wight County) d. 7/9/1797.

Children of Clements and Mary Hicks: Asa (3rd son) b. 9/1/1793; Rachal (1st daughter) b. 13/3/1795; Joseph (4th son) b. 10/11/1796.

Children of Thomas and Elizabeth Hunnicutt: Mary Ann b. 20/11//1799.

Children of John and Elizabeth Hamlin: Salley b. 28/10/1795; Phariba b. 30/9/1797; Lydia b. 5/8/1800.

Children of Josiah and Sarah Jordan: Ann Lutisha b. 5/3/1783; Jane Pleasants b. 14/8/1786.

James Jones of Sussex County d. 5/3/1793, 79 years old.

Children of Garrard and Sarah Ladd of Mecklinburg County: Agathia b. 6/1/1761; Elizabeth b. 5/7/1762; Priscilla b. 25/3/1764 d. 26/10/1766; Huldah b. 5/9/1765; Jacob b. 13/7/1767; Sarah b. 1/6/1769; Ursula b. 17/6/1771; Garrard b. 2/6/1773; Priscilla b. 2/1/1776; Lydia b. 8/9/1778; Esther b. 19/1/1782

William Ladd of Mecklinburg County d. 2/2/1780, 72 years old.

Robert Langley (member of Gravely Run Meeting) d. 27/9/1792.

Garrard (son of Garrard and Sarah Ladd) d. 23/1/1800.

Children of Jacob and Elizabeth Ladd: Ann b. 28/1/1799; Sarah Gilliam b. 8/4/1800.

Children of Peter and Obedianic Merimoon: Elizabeth b. 3/1/1760; Rhoda b. 3/12/1762; Robert b. 24/12/1763; Hannah b. 13/10/1766.

Children of Thomas Durham and Arebella Madkins: Daniel b. 24/5/1763; Sarah b. 19/2/1765; Esther b. 17/9/1767; William b. 25/12/1769; Martha b. 12/3/1772; Huldah b. 1/3/1774; Ann b. 12/3/1776; Mary b. 4/8/1779; Jane b. 25/12/1781; Thomas b. 1/10/1786; Ruth 7/4/1787.

Thomas D. Madkins d. 11 month, 1794.

Children of Barnaby and Sarah Nixon: Samuel b. 21/3/1781; David b. 7/12/1785.

Sarah (wife of Baraby Nixon and an Elder and member of Burleigh Meeting) d. 17/9/1799.

Children of William and Susanna Peebles: Huldah b. 21/9/1766 d. 28/8/1772; Butler b. 14/9/1770 struck dead by lightning d. 22/5/1775. Huldah Ladd (2nd daughter) b. 9/1/1774

Children of Peter and Mourning Peebles of Prince George County: Mordecai b. 19/9/1777; Josiah b, 25/12/1779; William Ladd b. 8/1/1782; Sarah b. 28/11/1785; Peter b. 12/4/1793

William Ladd Peebles d. 27/9/1786.

Peter and Huldah Peebles: Peter (2nd son) b. 7/5/1744.

Mourning Peebles (wife of Peter Peebles, daughter of William and Sarah Hargrave of Surry County) b. 29/4/1757.

Children of James and Benjamina Phillips: Samuel b. 2/11/1778; Henry and George b. 22/11/1779.

Children of James and Sarah Peebles: Ann b. 14/1/1781.

Children of John and Mary Peebles: Elizabeth b. 25/3/1778; Silviah b. 29/7/1780.

Children of William and Susanna Peebles: Anna b. 26/6/1776 d. 21/10/1780; Susanna b. 16/10/1778.

Huldah Ladd Peebles, daughter of William and Susanna Peebles, d. 12/9/1782.

Peter Peebles of Prince George County b. 28/7/1714.

Huldah Peebles (wife of Peter Peebles daughter of William Ladd of Charles City County) b. 13/2/1712.

Children of Peter and Huldah Peebles: William b. 17/1/1738.

Susanna Peebles (wife of William Peebles, daughter of Joseph and Ann Butler of Dinwiddie County) b. 14/4/1749.

William Peebles d. 30/12/1781, bur. 1/1/1782

Children of John and Mary Peebles: Margreat (3rd daughter) b. 16/9/1782; Micajah b. 19/2/1785; William b. 3/9/1787 d. 8/5/1793; Deborah (4th daughter) b. 20/12/1789 d. 29/10/1791; Sarah b. 20/6/1792.

Children of James and Sarah Peebles: Elijah b. 12/2/1783; Penninah b. 16/5/1785 d. 30/9/1785; Penninah (3rd daughter) b. 19/2/1787; Samuel b. 14/4/1789; Lucy (4th daughter) b. 19/3/1791.

Huldah Peebles (wife of Peter Peebles) d. 6/6/1784, about 72 years old.

Peter Peebles, Sr. d. 2/4/1794, 80 years old.

Children of Thomas and Anne Pritlow: Samuel b. 28/7/1784; Thomas b. 16/8/1786; Joshua b. 26/4/1788.

Elizabeth (wife of Stephen Peebles) d. 6/8/1788.

Children of Stephen and Sarah Peebles: Mary b. 27/10/1791; Elisha b. 20/4/1793; William Scott b. 24/9/1796; Elizabeth b. 15/10/1799 d. 18/2/1800; John b. 25/3/1801

Samuel Peebles (2nd son of James and Sarah Peebles) d. 4/10/1793.

Children of James and Sarah Peebles: Deborah (5th daughter) b. 17/6/1793; Samuel (3rd son) b. 11/9/1795; John (4th son) b. 13/5/1798

John Peebles d. 3/6/1796.

Peter Peebles (Elder and member of Burleigh Meeting) d. 1/1/1801.

Children of Thomas and Anne Pritlow: Sarah 5/5/1790; John b. 5/10/1792; Joseph b. 27/10/1794; Robert b. 19/1/1797; Anselm b. 4/5/1799; Mary Anne 1/2/1801. Anne Pritlow (wife of Thomas Pritlow) d. 2/8/1802.

Margaret Bailey (dau. of Samuel Bailey) d. 3/9/1802.

James Peebles d. 24/4/1810.

Children of Benjamin and Mourning Russel of Sussex County: Phebe b. 26/8/1778 d. 2/3/1787; Lemuel b. 19/11/1780 d. -/2/1781; Sophia b. 1/3/1783; Rebecca b. 9/7/1785; Benjamin Bailey (3rd son, 2nd son dies without name) b. 9/6/1788 d. 6/10/1789.

Children of Benjamin and Faith Bailey; Mourning b. 22/1/1750.

Benjamin Russel of Cumberland County, Old England now member of this meeting b. 20/4/1736.

Mourning Russel (wife of Benjamin Russel) d. 13/10/1789.

Children of Edward and Mary Stabler of Petersburg: Edward b. 25/7/1758 d. 2/1/1768 in Wilmington, PA; Sarah b. 7/3/1760 d. 29/7/1762 (buried in Friends Burying Ground at Curles Meeting House; Ann b. 30/11/1763; Mary b. 27/11/1765; William b. 30/8/1767; Edward (3rd son) b. 28/9/1769.

Anderson Simmons, of Prince George County, b. 17/1/1726.

Children of Anderson and Tabitha Simmons: Elizabeth b. 14/11/1757.

Children of Samson and Ruth Stanton of Southampton County: James b. 9/1/1771; John b. 25/9/1772; Sarah b. 20/8/1774; Daniel b. 25/6/1776.

Children of Thomas and Martha Sadler of Brunswick County: William Rose, b. 14/12/1765; Bartley b. 17/1/1769; Nathaniel b. 13/1/1772; Lucy b. 5/7/1774; Thomas b. 1/12/1777.

Children of James and Ann Stanton of Dinwiddie County: John b. 7/10/1777; James b. 16/7/1779; William b. 16/11/1782; Frederec b. 7/2/1784; Mary b. 28/3/1786; Robert b. 17/7/1788.

Children of John and Sarah Sears: Paul b. 14/12/1768; Elizabeth b. 31/8/1770; Huldah b. 22/11/1772; John 4/2/1775; Sarah b. 21/9/1777; Martha b. 4/5/1780; Samuel Sears (3rd son) b. 14/8/1783; Peter and Anna b. 5/4/1787.

Mary Stabler (wife of Edward Stabler) d. 30/12/1780, buried at Friends Burying Ground at Gravelly Run Meeting House.

Christian Stanton (wife of James Stanton) d. 3/6/1783, about 90 years old.

Edward Stabler (Elder and member of Gravely Run) d. 23/6/1785.

Children of Charles and Rhoda Sadler: Sarah b. 31/8/1778 d. 19/1/1796; Benjamin b. 14/5/1780 d. 1/11/1788; John Smith b. 17/2/1782; Merianna b. 24/7/1785 d. 20/10/1788; Rebecca b. 9/1/1787; Miriam b. 2/3/1792.

James Stanton (Elder and member of Stanton Meeting) d. 4/1/1789, about 90 years old.

Tabitha Simmons (wife of Anderson Simmons) d. 3/1/1790, about 71 years old.

Child of James and Ann Stanton: Lemuel b. 14/12/1790.

Child of Anderson and Huldah Simmons: Deborah b. 7/11/1792.

Anderson Simmons d. 28/2/1793

Thomas Sadler d. 5/11/1794.

Child of Paul and Huldah Sears: Meriam b. 7/8/1795.

Children of Joseph and Rebecah Sebrel: Sally b. 9/6/1787; Benjamin b. 6/4/1789; Matthew b. 4/11/1791; Susan b. 25/1/1794; Joseph b. 15/4/1796; Polly b. 29/7/1798.

Child of John and Lydia Stanton: Elizabeth b. 12/9/1798.

Child of James and Ann Stanton: Mary Ann b. 5/6/1802; James Edwin b. 4/10/1804.

Children of William and Ursely Taylor: Cornelius b. 8/4/1766; Thomas b. 7/2/1771; Geering(?) (son) b. 4/2/1773.

Children of Christopher and Elizabeth Taylor of Mecklenburg County: Reuben b. 30/9/1782; Simson b. 2/6/1785; Ann b. 3/1/1787.

Children of James and Ann Watkins of Sussex County: Mary b. 10/11/1772; Sarah b. 22/12/1774; Susanna b. 9/2/1777; Reubin b. 13/5/1779.

Samuel Warren, Sr., of Surry County b. 24/5/1730.

Hannah Warren (wife of Samuel Warren) b. 6/4/1743.

Children of Samuel and Hannah Warren: Sarah b. 26/10/1760; Elizabeth b. 26/2/1763; John b. 9/9/1767; Samuel b. 19/9/1775.

Children of Timothy and Susanna Ward of Brunswick County: Kizia b. 18/10/1760; John b. 6/1/1765; Stephen b. 1/3/1771; Mary b. 23/8/1773; Obed b. 7/11/1776; Ruth b. 16/11/1779.

Children of John and Ann White: Lemuel b. 8/1/1776; Mary b. 12/1/1777; Phranky(?), b. 4/1/1779 d. 29/4/1781; Elizabeth b. 11/5/1780; Lucy b. 17/9/1781.

Children of Thomas and Elizabeth Walthall: Jane b. 18/12/1779; William Bott b. 38/1/1782.

Elizabeth Walthal (daughter of William and Susanna Bott) b. 25/6/1755.

Children of James and Ann Watkins: John (2nd son) b. 1/6/1781; Winney (4th daughter) b. 12/8/1784; James b. 28/6/1786; Benjamin b. 12/10/1788.

Susanna Ward (wife of Timothy Ward of Brunswick County) d. 25/12/1784.

Children of Thomas and Susannah Walthall: Francis b. 5/6/1786.

Richard Wren b. 28/7/1738.

Hannah Wren b. 28/7/1738.

Children of Richard and Hannah Wren: Evans b. 31/8/1763; William b. 26/2/1768; Sucky b. 22/1/1779; Sally b. 13/1/1788.

Susanna (2nd wife of Thomas Walthall of Dinwiddie County) d. 8/11/1788.

Children of Evans and Lucy Wren: Richard b. 4/4/1784; Elizabeth b. 4/1/1787; Elitha b. 22/11/1789; Fanny b. 22/6/1791 d. 12/9/1798; Alphred b. 18/10/1798.

Children of William and Lydia Wren: Julia b. 10/2/1793; Elijah b. 18/11/1796; Deborah b. 14/12/1799; Mary b. 22/9/1802; Anne b. 2/4/1805.

Richard Wren (Elder and member of Stanton Meeting) d. 30/1/1804.

Hannah Wren, wife of Richard Wren, d. 18/3/1804.

Children of John and Ann White: Benjamin (2nd son) b. 22/7/1783; Ann (5th daughter) b. 11/3/1785; Dazae (Dozae) b. 14/8/1787; Clotilda b. 19/5/1789.

Ann White (member of Seacock Meeting) d. 18/9/1806, about 49 years old. John White (member of Seacock Meeting) d. 6/10/1806. about 54 years old.

Minutes - Men's and Women's

The Men's minutes beginning in 1765 and continuous until 17/8/1799 and the Women's minutes, 1752 - 1775, resuming in 1792, have been combined here, reducing a certain amount of duplication. Marriage references have been omitted here from the minutes when the marriage appears as a separate entity elsewhere.

21/12/1752. At Blackwater, Surry Co. John Murdough and Sarah Sebral to marry. Saml. Pritlow and Mary Bailey to marry.

15/3/1753. Joseph Bailey and Mary Stanton to marry. Joseph Tharp and Anne West to marry.

21/9/1753. Tryal Bailey and Martha Kitchen to marry.

18/10/1753. Joseph Tharp and Anne West to marry.

18/4/1754. John Watkins and Jane Strange to marry.

21/11/1754. Robert Hunnicutt, Junr., and Anne Simmons to marry.

18/9/1755. Elijah Bailey and Lucy Brock to marry.

21/11/1755. Hartwell Hargrave and Miriam Bailey to marry.

19/2/1756. Elizabeth Clary disowned for her disorderly walking.

-/8/1756. Anderson Simmons and Tabitha Butler to marry.

21/10/1756. Benjamin Merriott and Mourning Cornwell to marry.

19/5/1757. Absalom Bailey and Elisabeth Hargrave to marry.

16/3/1758. Mary Binford disowned.

19/4/1759. Samuel Warren and Hannah Inman to marry.

15/5/1760. Martha Steaphenson petitioned to be received into membership [received].

15/1/1761. Thomas Denson and Elizabeth Little to marry.

17/3/1761. John Hunnicutt and Mary Butler to marry.

21/11/1761. Anselm Bailey, Junr., and Ruth Hunnicutt to marry.

20/2/1762. Martha Simmons disowned.

20/3/1762. William Outland and Ann Scott to marry.

18/12/1762. Jesse Henley and Ann Pretlow to marry.

15/1/1763. Caleb Trublood and Mourning Meriott to marry.

19/2/1763. Micajah Bailey and Elisabeth Cryer to marry.

19/3/1763. John Cornwell and Mary Cornwell to marry.

17/9/1763. Certificates for Mourning Trueblood and Eliza. Fowler to monthly meeting in Henrico and monthly meeting in Pasquotank Co., NC.

20/10/1764. Simmons Fowler and Mary Sears to Mary.

16/3/1765. Certificate for John Pretlow and wife prepared.

21/9/1765. Agness Peebles disowned.

20/12/1765. Marriage of William Peebles and Susannah Butler orderly accomplished. Joshua Storrs, atty for Samuel and Emannuel Elams, complains that Anselem Bailey and sons stands indebted to said Elam and dispute a payment.

19/7/1766. Certificate for John Fowler and wife received.

21/2/1767. Marriage of Thomas Ricks and Elizabeth Cornwell orderly accomplished; he was required to produce a certificate. Matthew Jones produced a certificate from Monthly Meeting at the Western Branch. Certificate for Elisabeth, wife of Thomas Ricks, to Western Branch. Certificate for Edward Stabler and Robert Langley with their families and Ann Atkinson from the meeting held in Henrico Co.

21/3/1767. Monthly meeting held at Burleigh in Prince George Co. 16/5/1767. Benjamin Crews produced a certificate from Henrico Monthly Meeting. A certificate for Margaret, wife of Benjamin Crew, to White Oak Swamp in Henrico Co.

Friends [Quakers] excused from attending musters or paying fines upon their producing a certificate from the monthly meeting to the Lieutenant or chief officer of the militia in each county. Certificates were prepared and brought to this meeting for approval.

Friends [Quakers] to wit for the county of <u>Prince George</u>: Robert Hunnicutt, Peter Peebles, Benjamin Chappell, Wm. Simmons, Anderson Simmons, Robt. Hunnicutt, Jur., Equilla Binford, Thomas Binford, John Hunnicutt, Equilla Binford, William Peebles, William Hunnicutt (son Peter), William Hunnicutt (son Robt.), Joseph Simmons, Robt. Hunnicutt (son of Wyle), James Hunnicutt, Thos. Hunnicutt, Peter Peebles, Junr., Wyke Hunnicut, Jur., John Peebles, James Binford and Jesse Hunnicutt.

For <u>Sussex Co.</u>: Glaister Hunnicutt, Steaphen Hamlin, Nathan Briggs, Elijah Bailey, Joseph Bailey, Edmund Bailey, Ebeden Bailey, John Cornwell, James Clarey and Jesse Hargrave.

<u>Southampton Co.</u>: Thomas Pretlow, Thos. Nudby, David Davis, John Smith, Jonathan Gay, Joshua Bailey, Absalom Bailey, Sampson Stanton and Matthew Jones.

<u>Isle of Wight Co.</u>: William Hallerwell, Thomas Scott and George Scott.

<u>Dinwiddie Co.</u>: William Butler and his son John and Joseph, John Butler, James Butler and Jos. Butler son of James, John Sears, Henry Fowler, John Fowler, Junr., Robert Langley and Edward Stabler.

<u>Surry Co.</u>: Saml. Pretlow, Samuel Warren, Aron Cornwell, Anselm Bailey, Junr., Benja. Bailey, Junr., John Bailey, Samuel Bailey, Michael Bailey, Joseph Hargrave, Junr., Amselm Hargrave, Hartwell Hargrave.

20/6/1767. Joseph Jones produced a certificate from Monthly Meeting of Isle of Wight Co. for himself and family, dated 25/4/1767. It was reported that Barnet Clary has frequently appeared at musters of the militia,

18/7/1767 at Burleigh, Prince George Co. Anselm Bailey, John Smith and John Cornwell to treat with Robert Atkinson and family for sundry disorders.

15/8/1767. Naomy Hargrave being removed to New Garden in NC requests certificate for self and family.

19/9/1767. Burleigh. Pheba Ogburn, William Mason and Anne Mason ask to become members.

Collection: Robt. Hunnicutt, Jr. - 2.6; Robt. Hunnicutt - 10.0; William Hunnicutt - 2.6; Benjmn. Chappel - 5.0; Peter Binford - 6.0; Anderson Simmons - 2.6; William Simmons - 5.0; John Hunnicutt - 5.0; William Hunnicutt - 5.0; John Smith - 5.0(?); John Butler - 2.6; John Scars - 2.6; James Watkins - 2.6; Sampson Stanton - 3.9; Wyke Hunnicutt - 5.0; Matthew Jones - 2.6; Joseph Jones - 2.6; James Butler - 2.6; John Butler, Junr. - 2.6; Collection: ; Hartwell Hargrave - 5.0; Steaphen Hamlin - 5.0; Joseph Bailey - 2.6; Benja. Bailey, Junr. - 5.0; Joseph Hargrave - 5.0; Anselm Bailey - 5.0; Joseph Butler - 5.0; John Cornwell - 2.6; Wyke Hunnicutt - 5.0

Mary Briggs seems inclined to join the Church of England; does not wish to remain a member of the Society. [disowned].

21/11/1767. Burleigh. Pheaby Ogburn d. a few days since. Edward Stabler and his family desire to join Gravelly Run Meeting. Anne Mason is received as a member.

19/12/1767. Collection: Elijah Bailey, Thomas Newby, Thos. Pretlow, Saml. Warren. Silviah Hargrave requests a certificate to monthly meeting at the Western Branch.

16/1/1768. A certificate from Henrico Monthly Meeting on behalf of the Friends that are members of the meeting held at Benjamin Pattison's in Amelia Co., to join them to this meeting and they are received: Benja. Pattison and his wife and their son Benja. and dau. Elisabeth; John Merrymoon and his wife, their sons, Davis, Francis and John and their daus. Margret and Hannah; Peter Merrymoon and his wife;

William Reams and his wife and his sons, Jeremiah and Hezekiah; William Pattison and his wife; William Bott and his wife. Joseph Butler, son of James, intends to marry a member of Western Branch Monthly Meeting and requests a certificate. Certificate from monthly meeting in Henrico for Elisabeth Pattison and her three daus.: Elisabeth, Margaret and Hannah Pattison; Obediance Merrimon; Kesiah Pattison; Susannah Bott; and Margaret Merrimon.

19/3/1768. Glaister Hunnicutt is appointed overseer for Burleigh in the place of Wyke Hunnicutt, dec'd; he is to keep a record of births and deaths of Friends.

16/4/1768. Marriage of Joseph Butler, son of Willm. and Meriam Hunnicutt, dau. of Robt., orderly accomplished. Sufferings of Friends; Seized from William Hallewell - 30; from Steaphen Hamlin - 25; from Anderson Simmons - 10. Samuel Bailey is given liberty to defend a suit at law.

20/8/1768. Black Water. Marriage of William Hunnicutt and Mary Binford orderly accomplished. James Butler, Junr. petitioned the meeting for a certificate for clearness in marriage to monthly meeting at the Western Branch.

17/9/1768. Joseph Watkins condemns his outgoing in marriage.

17/12/1768. Marriage of Aron Cornwell and Ann Clary orderly accomplished. Thomas Pretlow requests liberty to sue Thomas Duke in behalf of Thomas Newby's orphans.

31/1/1769. Mary Barker, dau. of John Barker, requests to be a member.

18/2/1769. A request was made for a certificate showing clearness of marriage for Matthew Jones to the Western Branch in the Isle of Wight Co. Jordan Clary and Prissilla Briggs to marry. [It appears that Priscilla Briggs's desire to come among Friends has only been since Jordan Clary made suit to her and the second declaration to marry is rejected.]

18/3/1769. Testimony of Sarah Hunnicutt and children concerning her husband, Wyke Hunnicutt, dec'd. Certificate from Monthly Meeting in Henrico Co. for William Ladd and his wife Ursley and their children: Elizabeth, Huldah, Jacob and James Ladd.

20/5/1769. It is recommended that the meeting held at Robert Langley's be joined to the meeting at Gravelly Run. Jarrad Ladd and his wife Sarah request to become members. Samuel Bailey complains that Thomas Pretlow is in his debt and neglects to make payment.

17/6/1769. A certificate directed to Rich Square Monthly Meeting in North Carolina for John Merrymoon and his wife and their sons, Francis and John, and their dau. Hannah; Peter Merrymoon and his wife; Jeremiah Reams and his wife. Informed that John Fowler, Junr. has for sometime past behaved very disorderly. Jordan Clary and Priscilla Briggs to marry.

15/7/1769. Accounts of orphans:
Michael Bailey's acct. for Josiah Hargrave; Peter Peebles's acct. for Elisabeth and Mourning Peebles; Thomas Pretlow's acct. for Thomas Pretlow, orphan of Joshua Pretlow; Ann Pretlow's acct for Rebekah Pretlow. It is understood that Thomas Newby is not yet of age and thought the account may not be justly settled the meeting is of the judgment that Thomas Pretlow, getting him to settle and sign the account before he is of age is unbecoming and may be dangerous precedent.

19/8/1769. Marriage of Robert Hunnicutt, son of Wyke, and Prissilla Hunnicutt orderly accomplished.

21/10/1769. John Pleasants produced a certificate from Henrico Monthly Meeting. John Pattison and family request a certificate to Rich Square, NC.

18/11/1769. To treat with Thomas Pretlow for defending at the suit at law. John Bailey requests a certificate signifying his clearness in marriage to Western Branch Monthly Meeting. Meriam Pleasants and her three daus., Meriam, Margreat and Ann Hunnicutt are about to removed within the verge of Henrico Monthly Meeting and request a certificate. Mary Barker received into membership.

20/1/1770. David Merrymoon petitions for a certificate for self and wife to monthly meeting at Rich Square in NC.

17/2/1770. All the Friends belonging to the meeting held at Benja. Pattison's are mostly removed, all but William Reams, William Bott and their families; therefore that meeting is discontinued. William Reams and family are joined to Gravelly Run Meeting. Joining William Bott to a meeting is deferred.

17/3/1770. Certificate for Benjamin Russil from Western Branch in the Isle of Wight Co. Timothy Ward of Brunswick Co. applied to be a member.

21/4/1770. Thomas Newby requests a certificate to the monthly meeting at the Western Branch signifying his clearness in marriage. 21/7/1770. William Bott informs the meeting that he and h's family choose to be members of Gravelly Run Particular Meeting.

18/8/1770. It is reported that a young woman has sworn a bastard child to Anselm Hargrave, a member of this meeting; he denies the fact.

20/10/1770. Anselm Hargrave disowned. Certificate requested for Willm. Reams and his wife to monthly meeting at Rich Square, NC.

16/3/1771. Ebiden (Abidan) Bailey and Sarah Sears to marry.

20/4/1771. Certificate for Matthew Kitchen from monthly meeting at the Western Branch. Anselm Bailey, Junr. replaces Joseph Hargrave as Treasurer. Informed that Wallis Butler (a professed member) has been guilty of sundry disorders and has got married by a hireling priest. Disowned.

21/5/1771. Marriage of Abiden Bailey and Sarah Sears orderly accomplished. Spoke to William Butler respecting the conduct of his son Wallace (marrying out).

15/6/1771. Reported that Matthew Kitchen has no estate and is incapable of maintaining himself and it is agreed that David Davis will board him the present year at the rate of £3. Wallis Butler disowned.

17/8/1771. Marriage of Jesse Hargraves and Susannah Hamlin orderly accomplished.

19/10/1771. Reported that John Fowler, Senr. is in want of some relief. Timothy Ward to be received as a member but as he lives remote from any particular meeting he is desired to attend this meeting as often as is convenient.

21/12/1771. Charles Clary requests a certificate to monthly meeting at the Western Branch signifying his clearness in marriage. Benjamin Russel requests a certificate to monthly meeting at Cedar Creek in Hanover Co.

15/2/1772. George Scott applied for leave to sue for a Negro slave which he thinks is withheld from him unjustly.

18/4/1772. John Walker of Great Britain sent a letter to the meeting requesting assistance in settling an account with Robert Langley. Sufferings: Seized from Edward Stabler - 12; from Sam Bailey - 45; from Joseph Hargrave - 110; from Samson Stanton - 21; from James Stanton - 35.6. Overseer to be appointed in the place of Anselm Bailey, dec'd., for Black Water Particular Meeting.

16/5/1772. James Hunnicutt produced a certificate from monthly meeting in Caroline Co. Sufferings: Seized from William Simmons - 28; from Anderson Simmons - 9; from Peter Peebles - 12; Sarah Hunnicutt - 25; William Hunnicutt - 5.6; Robert Hunnicutt - 20.

20/6/1772. Marriage of James Hunnicutt and Rebekah Pretlow orderly accomplished; attended by Eliza. Bailey, wife of Benja. Bailey and Mary Bailey, wife of John Bailey.

18/7/1772. William Mason stands charged with sundry disorders; has neglected meetings.

19/9/1772. Robert Hunnicutt, Senr., and Agness Chappel to marry. Thomas Binford requests certificate to monthly meeting at White Oak

Swamp in Henrico Co. signifying his clearness in marriage.
21/11/1772. Marriage of John Smith and James Brock orderly accomplished. Thomas Newby requests certificate to the monthly meeting at the Western Branch.
19/12/1772. Thomas Sadler of Brunswick Co. requests to become a member.
16/1/1773. William Mason disowned. Sarah Ladd requests to be a member. Reported that Jonathan Gay has been guilty of sundry disorders - disowned. Robert Hunnicutt and Agnes Chappel not proceeding in their intended marriage as declared; dropped by mutual consent.
15/5/1773. Marriage of James Binford and Elisabeth Simmons orderly accomplished. [witnessed by Mary Hunnicutt, wife of William, son of Peter and Mary Hunnicutt, wife of William son of Robert].
19/6/1773. William Ladd produced a certificate signifying his clearness in marriage from monthly meeting at White Oak Swam in Henrico Co.
17/7/1773. Marriage of William Ladd and Mary Hunnicutt orderly accomplished.
21/8/1773. Hezekiah Reams has almost wholly neglected meetings. Mary Ladd is removed by marriage within Henrico Monthly Meeting. A certificate is requested.
18/9/1773. Christian Stanton, aged and infirm, requests to be discharged from acting as an overseer in Stanton Meeting, recommending Faitha Stanton as her replacement.
20/11/1773. Benjamin Russel proposing to return and settle within the verge of this meeting, produced a certificate from monthly meeting at Cedar Creek and Caroline. Ann Thompson, late Mason, is married by a hireling priest - disowned.
16/12/1773. Robert Evens of Petersburg requests to be taken into membership. Ann Thompson (late Mason) disowned.
15/1/1774. Hezekiah Reams has married out and does not desire to be under the care of Friends. Disowned.
19/3/1774. Thomas Hunnicutt by his brother Robert requests a certificate to monthly meeting at Cain Creek, NC. David Fisher request to become a member.
19/5/1774. Ruth Binford, wife of Thos., late a member of monthly meeting at White Oak Swamp in Henrico Co. and now removed and settled within the limits of this monthly meeting, produced a certificate.
20/8/1774. Hannah White produced a certificate from the monthly meeting at White Oak Swamp in Henrico Co.

15/10/1774. Matthew Harris of Isle of Wight Co. requests to become a member. Mary House requests to be received as a member.

9/11/1774. Marriage of Joshua Bailey and Patience Stanton orderly accomplished.

21/1/1775. John White and Ann Cornwell to marry. Matthew Harris and Mary House to marry. William Butler and Joseph Butler, son of James, are appointed to assist Women Friends in preparing a certificate for Jane Watkins, widow of John Watkins, dec'd. [to monthly meeting at Rich Square, NC]. David Fisher and Martha Butler to marry.

18/3/1775. Steaphen Hamlin one of the overseers for Stanton Meeting being dec'd. a replacement is sought.

15/4/1775. Lemuel Bailey requests a certificate to monthly meeting at the Western Branch signifying his clearness in marriage. Anselm Hargrave requests a certificate to monthly meeting at the Western Branch signifying his clearness in marriage. Mary Bailey, an Elder, a member of Black Water particular Meeting, d. 27/2/1775. Steaphen Hamlin, an Elder, a member of Stanton's Meeting, d. 3rd month 1775. Sufferings: John Butler - 20; from Edward Stabler - 18/8; from Sampson Stanton - 24.

20/5/1775. Tryal Bailey received as a member.

16/9/1775. Sarah Pinner, dau. of Robt. Scott, dec'd., of the Isle of Wight Co., disowned in that she hath been ensnared with a wicked man, joyn in carnal copulation with him and when big with child by him quit him by and would not have him and married with an other. Patience Jordan, dau. of Richd. Jordan of Isle of Wight Co., disowned for taking her cousin to be her husband. Elizabeth Denson, dau. of William Denson of the Isle of Wight Co., disowned. Elizabeth Sebrell disowned for committing fornication.

21/10/1775. Marriage of Steaphen Butler and Elisabeth Hunnicutt orderly accomplished. Benjamin Johnson and Rebeckah Pretlow to marry.

7/11/1775. Benjamin Johnson produced certificate from monthly meeting in Henrico signifying his clearness in marriage.

16/12/1775. Christopher Anthony and Mary Jordan to marry. Aron Cornwell requests certificate for self and wife to monthly meeting at Wellses, Perquimons Co., NC.

[... pages missing ...]

9th month 1776 ... James Stanton, son of Silvanus, received as a member to the Gravelly Run Preparative Meeting. Thomas Hunnicutt produced certificate from the monthly meeting at Cain Creek in NC.

19/10/1776. James Stanton, Junr. and Ann Butler to marry. John Butler, son of Joseph, requests a certificate to monthly meeting at the Western Branch signifying his clearness in marriage.

19/6/1779. Informed by Blackwater Meeting that John Bailey, Joseph G. Bailey and Thos. Pretlow (son of Joshua) had hired substitutes to act for them in the militia on a certain occasion. [John Bailey was disowned.] William Butler and Faith Stanton to marry. Stephen Butler produced Mary Fowler's account for boarding and cloathing John Fowler for one year. Certificate produced from monthly meeting at White Oak Swamp for Gerrard Ladd.

18/9/1779. Marriage of William Butler orderly accomplished. Robert Atkinson received into membership.

16/10/1779. John Butler, son of Jas., declared his intentions of marriage with Elizabeth Stanton. Friends in Brunswick Co. report that James Ladd voluntarily bears arms and says he shall continue to do so. Recommended as Elders: William Hunnicutt, son of Robt., Lucy Bailey, Ann Hunnicutt, wife of Robt. and Ann Hunnicutt, wife of Wyke.

20/11/1779. Gerrard Ladd requests certificate to the Lieutenant of the Mecklenburg Co. [re militia service].

18/12/1779. Informed that Benjamin Bailey, son of Anselm, has voluntarily contributed towards hiring persons to serve in a military capacity.

15/1/1780. James Ladd disowned. Reported that John Butler, son of Jas. hath engaged the affections of a woman not of our Society in expectation of marriage and whilst under that engagement, attempted to marry another. Benjamin Bailey disowned.

18/3/1780. Informed by letter from Henrico Monthly Meeting that a suit at law was commenced against the executors of Ellyson Crews, dec'd., for a division of the Negroes belonging to that estate, and that it was ordered by Thomas Binford, a member of this meeting, the sd. Binford being present, not appearing willing to say he will dismiss the suit at present, but requests further time to consider of it. James Peebles and Sarah Bailey, dau. of Elijah, to marry.

15/4/1780. Reported from Gravelly Run Meeting that John Butler, son of Jas., has lately taken a wife contrary to discipline - disowned. By report from Stanton Meeting, Bannester Betts request to be received into membership. Samuel Pretlow request certificate re clearness in marriage to Perquimons Monthly Meeting in NC. John Butler, son of Joseph, and Martha his wife, having again removed within the limits of this meeting, produced certificate from Western Branch Monthly Meeting. Sufferings: Taken from John Butler, son of Wm. - 14 barls.

corn; Joseph Butler, son of Wm. - 4 barls. of corn; John Butler, son of Jos. - 2 barls. of corn; Ann Butler 9 barls. of corn; Wm. Butler - £6; David Fisher - £3.8; Stephen Butler - 1 gun; Robt. Hunnicutt, senr. - 1 horse and 2 beds; Peter Peebles, senr. - 1 horse; Anderson Simmons - be and furniture and 1 barrl. corn; John Hunnicutt - 2 barrls. corn; Wm. Simmons - 1 blanket and 3 sheets; Wm. Hunnicutt - 1 bed and some furniture; Jas. Binford - 1 horse and 2 barrls. corn; Peter Cappell Binford - 1 mare, 3 barrls corn and 1 bed and furniture; Wyke Hunnicutt - 1 mare; Thos. Hunnicutt - 3 barrls. corn; Barnaby Nixon - 1 sheet; Robt. Hunnicutt, son of Peter - 1 bed and furniture; Joseph Simmons - 1 bedd; Wm., Peebles - 1 bed and some furniture.

John Butler, son of Jas. disowned; also Elizabeth Stanton his now wife.

27/5/1780. Thomas Binford, son of Peter, disowned. Mary Fowler to be paid £8 for boarding John Fowler.

17/6/1780. Marriage of James Peebles orderly accomplished.

15/7/1780. Reported from blackwater Meeting that Absolom Bailey [son of Benja. Bailey of Southampton Co.] has married a woman not of the Society, by a priest - disowned. Robert Atkinson and Martha Clary to marry. Banister Betts is received into membership. Josiah Jordan, Junr. and Sarah Hunnicutt to marry. Jacob Cornwell having removed to NC, requests certificate to monthly meeting at Simons Creek.

16/9/1780. Marriage of Robert Atkinson orderly accomplished. Josiah Jordan, Junr. produced certificate from monthly meeting at Western Branch.

21/10/1780. Wards Meeting in Brunswick Co. reports that William Taylor request to be received into membership. Christopher Taylor of Mecklinburg Co. requests to be received into membership. Thomas Binford condemns his misconduct and is received into membership again.

20/1/1781. Jacob Cornwell sent in a paper to the meeting acknowledging that he had through a sudden fright fired several guns at a privateer which attached a vessel he was in when at sea.

17/2/1781. Informed that Charles Hamlin is about to marry a woman Friend in NC and requests a certificate purporting his clearness of other marriage engagements. James Hicks, Edwin Ellis, William Hicks and Clements Hicks, having for a considerable time been diligent attenders of our religious meetings and of orderly conduct, did sometime since petition to be received into membership. Joseph Denson having removed within the verge of Western Branch Monthly Meeting requests a certificate.

17/3/1781. Samuel Cornwell and Sarah Bailey, dau. of Saml., to marry. Brunswick Meeting recommends that Thos. Durham Madkin be received into membership. Elizabeth Ladd, dau. of Jarrot Ladd, being about to remove within the compass of Rich Square Monthly Meeting, NC, requests certificate.

21/4/1781. Informed that Ann Stabler and Mary Stabler, daus. of Edward Stabler, are removed within the compass of the monthly meeting at Fairfax in Loudoun Co. and a certificate is requested. Sufferings (chiefly for military requisition): Robert Hunnicutt, senr. - horse and bed and 1 sheet; Peter Peebles, senr., 1 feather bed and furniture; John Peebles - 1 stone candle stand & 1 slate; John Hunnicutt - 1 horse; Wm. Hunnicutt - 1 mare; Peter Peebles, Junr. - 3 sheet and 1 bolster; Barnaby Nixon - 1 dish, 1 bason and 2 plates; Wyke Hunnicutt - 1 horse; Anderson Simmons - 1 mare and 1 looking glass; Wm. Simmons - 1 horse; James Binford - 1 bed and furniture; James Peebles - 1 coffy mill and 1 blanket; Wm. Peebles - 1 mare; Chappel Binford - 1 horse; Joseph Simmons - 1 horse, 2 dishes and 6 plates; Thos. Binford (son of Thos.) - 1 case of bottles and 3 gallons brandy; Thos. Binford, senr. - 2 beds, 2 sheets and 1 blanket; Agness Chappel - 1 horse; Robt. Hunnicutt (son of Peter) - 1 horse; Mary Binford - 10 sheep; Wm. Butler - 1 cow; Wm. Hunnicutt - 1 cow; Jas. Butler - 1 cow; John Butler (son of Wm.) - 1 cow; Friends of the Weekday Meeting at Watkins - 6.11.3; Friends of Wards Meeting - 11.3.0.

17/5/1781. Certificate requested for Christopher Taylor to monthly meeting at Rich Square in NC regarding his clearness in marriage engagements. Hardy Crew of Caswell Co. in NC and Daniel Madkins of Mecklenburg Co., request to be received into membership.

16/6/1781. Money raised for payment to Mary Fowler. Informed that Denny (Demy?) Bailey has voluntarily served as a soldier.

15/9/1781. John Andrews requests to be received into membership [received]. William Butler an overseer of Gravelly Run being removed from said meeting is replaced by Stephen Butler.

21/10/1781. Josiah Cook produced certificate from Western Branch Monthly Meeting in Isle of Wight Co. Nicholas Jarrot and Richard Wrenn request to be received into membership.

15/12/1781. Reported that Pleasants Hunnicutt had been active in impressing beef grain for the use of the Army [acting as deputy commissary]. A request has been made for the division of the estate of Benjamin Chappel agreeable to his last will. Informed that Glaister Hunnicutt by his last will gave the following Negroes to this meeting: Tom, Joe, Ben, Charles, Jenny and Charlet directing that they be manumitted.

19/1/1782. Robert Ricks and Ann Pretlow to marry. James Binford and his wife are removed within the limits of Rich Square Monthly Meeting in NC; a certificate is requested.

16/2/1782. Pleasants Hunnicutt disowned. Robert Ricks produced a certificate from monthly meeting at the Western Branch signifying his clearness in marriage.

16/3/1782. Marriage of Ricks orderly accomplished.

20/4/1782. James Binford has not settled his affairs but expects to do so soon.

15/6/1782. Certificate prepared for James Binford and wife. Jacob Cornwell having settled within the limits of this meeting again, condemns his misconduct.

20/7/1782. John Andrews and Jane Hunnicutt to marry. Certificate requested for Thomas Binford, Junr. being removed within the limits of Henrico Monthly Meeting.

17/8/1782. Peter Binford and Martha Fowler to marry. Benja. Hunnicutt is guilty of card playing and horse racing and intends marriage with a woman not of our Society. Certificate for Josiah Jordan, Junr., produced from monthly meeting at Western Branch. Jonathan Coker and Wm. Linear request to be received into membership.

21/9/1782. Marriage of John Andrews orderly accomplished. Benjamin Hunnicutt disowned. David Fisher intends to visit his relations in New Jersey.

19/10/1782. Marriage of Peter Binford orderly accomplished. The following refuse to manumit their slaves: James Butler, an Elder to leave his Negroes free at his death and appears to give them up shortly; Sarah Hamlin, an Elder, Ann Hamlin, Charles Hamlin, Sarah Wilkerson, Joseph Simmons, Thos. Binford, Jane Hunnicutt, Leml. Bailey and Anselm Hargrave refuse to emancipate their slaves. John Hunnicutt refuses until he is further satisfied re the Act of Assembly. Martha Hargrave is agreeable but is concerned for their support. Elizabeth Langley and her daus. refuse, saying they cannot subsist without them. Ussula Ladd has but one and he refuses to be emancipated saying that he has as much freedom as he desires. Edwin Ellis, Nicholas Jarrott and Thomas Sadler say their wives are not willing, having only such as came by them. Agness Chappell refuses to emancipate her Negroes saying she had none longer than life, and her children can't do anything with their's till they are divided some of them not being of age.

16/11/1782. Lewis Dupress, Arabella Madkins, Medion Atkinson, Keziah

Taber and James Williams request to become members.

21/12/1782. Regarding complaints against Thomas Binford: it appears he endeavored to defend himself by blows, and got his gun with threats to shoot the man's horse but was prevented by some, and has brought suit against the man. He claims a crescent saw which he and one of his neighbours bought between them, intimating since his neighbour's death that he the longest liver has a right to the whole, which causes much discord between him and his neighbour. Edward Stabler informed this meeting that he intends to put his two sons, Wm. and Edwd. Stabler to school within the compass of Pipe Creek Monthly Meeting in Maryland. Tryall Bailey having removed within the limits of Western Branch Monthly Meeting request a certificate for himself and family.

15/2/1783. Thomas Binford, Junr., son of Thomas Binford of Prince George Co., disowned for overlooking slaves, distilling of grain and other disorders. A certificate produced for Tryall Bailey, his wife and children, Martha, Mourning and Joel, to Western Branch Monthly Meeting.

15/3/1783. Reported that Samuel Pretlow hath for some time has been in the practice of dancing and divers other things inconsistent with our profession. Accounts produced for the boarding and cloathing of John Fowler.

19/4/1783. Eliza. Judkins, late Warren, disowned, having married a man not in religious fellowship with our Society. Aaron Cornwell and his wife having again removed within the compass of this meeting, produced a certificate from monthly meeting at Wells(?), NC. Samuel Pretlow, son of Saml., of Surry Co., disowned.

21/6/1783. Blackwater Meeting reports that Joseph Cornwell has sold a slave, and that Jacob Cornwell and Sarah Wilkerson have married contrary to discipline - disowned.

19/7/1783. Thomas Pretlow, Junr., and Ann Bailey to marry.

20/9/1783. Marriage of Thos. Pretlow orderly accomplished. Thomas Binford, son of Peter Binford, of Prince George Co., disowned for falling into a passion with one of his neighbours and came to blows without manifesting a sincere sorrow. Joseph Crew Cornwell of Surry Co. disowned for divers disorders. James Judkins and Martha Stanton to marry.

18/10/1783. James Judkins produced a certificate from monthly meeting at Rich Square in Northampton Co., NC, signifying his clearness in marriage.

15/11/1783. Marriage of Jas. Judkins orderly accomplished.

20/12/1783. Joseph Bailey, son of Jos., and Sarah Hunnicutt, dau. of Wm., to marry.

17/1/1784. Gravelly Run Meeting reports that Joseph Butler, son of Jas. is removed within the limits of Rich Square Monthly Meeting in NC, and John Butler, son of Joseph, is within the limits of Western Branch Monthly Meeting - both without certificates.

21/2/1784. Marriage of Joseph Bailey orderly accomplished. Informed that Edwin Ellis is about to remove and settle within the limits of monthly meeting in Dobs Co., NC, and a certificate is requested. Wm. Hix disowned. Edward Ellis has not yet settled his affairs. Received into membership: Lewis Durpice, Arabella Madkins and Keziah Tabor; Median Atkinson being held up in that she has been in some intaglement particularly respecting some slaves. It appears that Wm. Bailey and Edward Bailey, sons of Benja., have been guilty of drinking to excess, swearing and other unwarrantable conduct - disowned. It is reported that Silas Hargrave has sometime since removed and settled within the limits of the Western Branch Monthly Meeting - certificate prepared.

19/6/1784. Reported by Blackwater Meeting that Joseph Glaister Bailey has contrary to advice of Friends, married by a priest to a person not of our Society [disowned].

17/7/1784. Ann Briggs has sold slaves - disowned.

21/8/1784. Burleigh Meeting reports that Josiah Jordan, Junr., a member of that meeting, has commenced a suit at law against a member of our Society.

18/9/1784. Certificate for John Crew and his wife Judith and children: Charles, Martha, Caleb and Joshua, from monthly meeting at Rich Square, Northampton Co., NC.

20/11/1784. William Stabler, son of Edward Stabler, has returned from school within the compass of Pipe Creek Monthly Meeting.

18/12/1784. Sarah Holleman condemns her outgoing in marriage. Josiah Jordan disowned. Wards Meeting reports that Lewis Dupree has married contrary to discipline - disowned. Certificate for Gerrot Robt. Ellyson, his wife and children: Darcus and Elijah, to Blackwater Meeting.

15/1/1785. Stephen Peebles and Elizabeth Chappel to marry. Gravelly Runn Meeting reports that Jos. Butler and his wife [Priscilla] and four children, Penniah, Ann, Mary and Jesse, are removed within the verge of the Western Branch Monthly Meeting and request a certificate. Reported by Burleigh Meeting that the conduct of Joseph Simmons has been reproachful, especially that of frequenting the company of a woman of a base character.

19/2/1785. William Meriott and Mary Cornwell to marry. Joseph Simmons has been guilty of drinking to excess. Informed that Daniel Butler has removed within the limits of the Western Branch Monthly Meeting without a certificate. Mary Nicholson, late Hargrave, disowned. John and Stephen Butler produced their account for boarding John Fowler.

19/3/1785. Marriage of Stephen Peebles orderly accomplished. Daniel Butler holds a Negro in a state of slavery. Burleigh Meeting reports that Robt. Hunnicutt, Junr., hath sold Negroes contrary to Discipline - disowned. Botts Meeting discontinued. Joseph Simmons of Prince George Co. disowned.

16/7/1785. A certificate for Daniel Butler directed to the monthly meeting of the Western Branch was produced to this meeting and approved. Thomas Walthall and Susanah Peebles to marry. Committee appointed to assist in the settlement of Benjamin Chappell's estate. Stanton Meeting is satisfied with receiving as members: Evans Wren, his wife Lucy, Hannah (wife of Richard) and Wm. Wren (their son). Wm. Linear has removed and settled within the verge of Rich Square Monthly Meeting, NC; a certificate is requested.

15/10/1785. Robert Bailey [son of Michl.] acknowledged his swearing and frequenting places of diversion and merriment and shows no disposition to condemn his conduct - disowned. Blackwater Meeting reports that Benjamin Bailey, son of Absalom, has for some time withdrawn himself from the Society and has lately married a wife not in membership - disowned. Wards Meeting informs that Hezikiah Tabour has for sometime past been in the practice of appointing meetings contrary to the Discipline. Certificate requested for Timothy Ward and his family to Center in Randolph Co., NC.

17/12/1785. John Andrews and Sarah Butler to marry. The certificate for Wm. Linear was not accepted by Rich Square Monthly Meeting, he having married out of unity of Friends - disowned.

9/2/1786. Wards Meeting desirous to move to Henry Sadler's, about 3 miles away. Reports from Burleigh Meeting of Glaister Hunnicutt swearing, gaming and dancing.

18/2/1786. Certificate for children of Joseph Butler, dec'd.: Elizabeth, James, Tilmon, Martha, Mary, Robt., Ann, Prissa and Jane, from monthly meeting at Rich Square in NC.

18/3/1786. Reported by Blackwater Meeting that Wm. Merriott has lately carried to Carolina several Negroes belonging to his brother John Meriott, in doing which he has been guilty of fraudulent and dishonest conduct [disowned].

27/5/1786. Reported from Burleigh Meeting that Jesse Binford has married a woman not professing with us.

17/6/1786. Reported from Gravelly Run Meeting that Wm. Fowler has for some time much neglected meetings and has been guilty of drinking to excess, using profane words and quarreling and fighting. Certificate for Richd. Hargrave from monthly meeting at Western Branch.

15/7/1786. Glaister Hunnicutt, son of the late Glaister Hunnicutt, disowned for dancing and gaming. Jesse Binford, son of Thos. Binford of Prince George Co. disowned for marrying a wife contrary to Discipline. William Fowler of Dinwiddie Co. disowned for declining attending religious meeting, drinking to excess, using profane words, quarreling and fighting.

19/8/1786. Reported by Blackwater Meeting Herman Hargrave has been guilty of criminal conversation with a young woman who charges him with being the father of her child [disowned]. Certificate for Samuel Hargrave, son of Jos. Hargrave, dec'd., from the Western Branch Monthly Meeting.

16/9/1786. William Stabler, being about to remove within the limits of Fairfax Monthly Meeting, requests a certificate.

21/10/1786. Certificate from Henrico Monthly Meeting for Hannah Ladd of Mecklinburg Co. and five of her children: Thomas, Judith, John, Amos and Joseph. Recommended as Elders: Wm. Bott, Sarah Nixon, Sarah Sears, Mourning Peebles, Ann Cornwell and Richd. Wrenn.

18/11/1786. William Ellzey and Agathy Ladd to marry.

16/12/1786. Wm. Ellzey produced a certificate from Rich Square Monthly Meeting in NC setting forth his clearness in marriage. John Butler and Selah (Cely) Hargrave to marry.

20/1/1787. Marriage of Wm. Ellzey orderly accomplished. John Butler, son of Jos. condemns his misconduct in marrying out.

17/2/1787. Marriage of John Butler orderly accomplished.

18/5/1787. Not quite easy to receive John Butler , son of Jas. John Stanton, son of Samson, being removed to within the limits of the Western Branch Monthly Meeting, requests a certificate.

21/7/1787. Certificate for Daniel Butler from Western Branch Monthly Meeting. Blackwater Meeting informs of difference between John Cornwell and Eliza. Cornwell, his mother-in-law.

15/9/1787. John White of NC and Mourning Cornwell to marry. Thomas Horn produced a certificate from monthly meeting Contentay, NC.

20/10/1787. John White produced a certificate from monthly meeting at Wellses in NC certifying his clearness in marriage engagements.

17/11/1787. Lazarus Johnson and Mary Hunnicutt to marry. Marriage of John White orderly accomplished. Informed that Christopher Taylor of Mecklenburg Co. intends to move with his family within the limits of Rich Square Monthly Meeting in NC and requests a certificate.

15/12/1787. Lazarus Johnson produced a certificate from monthly meeting at the Western Branch signifying his clearness in marriage engagements. Francis White of NC and Mary Simons to marry. Mary Hart, late Pretlow, disowned.

19/1/1788. Francis White produced a certificate from monthly meeting at Welles NC, signifying his clearness of marriage engagements.

16/2/1788. Marriage of Francis White and Mary Simons orderly accomplished. John Pretlow produced a certificate from Western Branch Monthly Meeting. Silas Hargrave and family being removed within the limits of this meeting produced a certificate from the Western Branch Monthly Meeting for himself and dau. Sally, and they with his wife and other children recommended to the care of Blackwater Meeting.

15/3/1788. John Cornwell requests certificate to monthly meeting at Wellses in NC in relation to marriage. Informed by Women Friends that Elizabeth Langley and her daus., Margaret and Elizabeth Langley, Jane Hunnicutt and Sarah Jordan, continue to hold slaves.

19/4/1788. Nathaniel Briggs, a minister and member of Stanton Meeting, d. 16/3/1788. The following members after being repeatedly visited, continue to hold slaves: John White, Anselm hargrave, Lemuel Bailey and Nicholas Jarad. Wyke Hunnicutt, one of the overseers of Burleigh, being removed within the compass of Gravelly Run Meeting, Wm. Hunnicutt is recommended for that station.

24/5/1788. Certificate for Mary White, late Simons to monthly meeting at Wellses in NC.

21/6/1788. Certificate for Ann Cornwell and children: Wm., Elizabeth, Jacob, Moses and Aaron Cornwell to monthly meeting at Wellses in NC. John Cornwell having removed within the limits of the monthly meeting at Wellses in NC, requests certificate. Lemuel Bailey still refuses to liberate his slaves.

19/7/1788. It appears that Saml. Butler is removed within the limits of the Western Branch Monthly Meeting; a certificate is requested.

16/8/1788. James Binford and Ann Pretlow to marry.

20/9/1788. Reported that James Hargrave [son of Hartwell Hargrave] has married a wife contrary to the rules of the Society [disowned].

18/10/1788. Lemuel Bailey intends to liberate his Negroes. Informed from Gravelly Run Meeting that David Fisher had hired a slave for one year and was active in selling a Negro [disowned]. Informed that Thos. Ladd, son of John, has married contrary to the rules of the Society - disowned.

15/11/1788. Clements Hicks and Mary Bailey, dau. of Jos., to marry. Elijah Bailey requests a certificate to the monthly meeting at Cain Creek in NC relative to marriage.

20/12/1788. Reported by Gravelly Run Meeting that Hezekiah Tabor has refrained attending Friend's meeting as well as his family; also has commenced a suit at law with a Friend and is unjust in his dealings [disowned]. Daniel Madkins doth much neglect the attendance meetings and has enlisted as a soldier and doth frequent and join with others gathered for vain amusements [disowned].

17/1/1789. Marriage of Clements Hicks orderly accomplished.

21/2/1789. Certificate for Margaret Heavenridge from monthly meeting at Cain Creek, NC. Certificate for Ann Henly purporting her being a member when she removed from these parts directed to the monthly meeting at Center in NC, approved. Certificate for Mahlon Budd from Philadelphia Monthly Meeting.

21/3/1789. Absolam Bailey condemned his previous misconduct as was received into membership. Blackwater Meeting reports that Robert Atkinson consented to his dau. marrying a man not in membership with us, giving a wedding dinner in his own house.

18/4/1789. Certificate for Mary Johnson to monthly meeting at the Western Branch. Stanton Meeting reports that Michael Bailey continues as a county court clerk. Certificate for Samuel Ricks from monthly meeting of the Western Branch.

20/6/1789. Robt. Atkinson acknowledges that he had acted contrary to the Discipline in consenting to his dau. in law having a wedding in his house.

18/7/1789. Stanton Meeting reports that Nicholas Jarrad, after executing manumissions for his slaves has since refused to allow them to go free, demanding the return of the manumissions which has been done; he is disowned. Elizabeth Langley (wife of Robt. Langley) and their daus. Margaret and Elizabeth disowned; also Jane Hunnicutt, widow of Glaister Hunnicutt, disowned - all for owning slaves. Certificate for Samuel Butler from monthly meeting at the Western Branch.

19/9/1789. Blackwater Meeting reports that David Davis has married contrary to Discipline.

17/10/1789. Aquilla Binford and Mary Chappel to marry. Abidon Bailey requests certificate to monthly meeting at White Oak Swamp in

Henrico Co. signifying his clearness in marriage.

21/11/1789. Blackwater Meeting reports that John Warrin has joined the Methodists and married a wife contrary to the rules of the Society - disowned. Informed that Mahlon Budd is about to remove back to Philadelphia and requests a certificate.

19/12/1789. Certificate for Samuel Hargrave is requested in order to marry. Jane Bailey produced a certificate from monthly meeting in Orange Co., NC.

16/1/1790. Thos. Walthal and Jemima Sears to marry. Michael Bailey disowned. Lemuel Bailey disowned. Blackwater Meeting reports that William Cornwell [son of John] has married a woman not in membership - disowned.

20/2/1790. Informed that Wm. Wren is removed within the verge of the Western Branch Monthly Meeting and requests a certificate. Informed that Samuel Ricks is removed within the verge of the Western Branch Monthly Meeting and requests a certificate. Reported that Anselm Hargrave is guilty of drinking to excess and absents himself from our religious meetings [disowned].

21/3/1790. Marriage of Thomas Walthal orderly accomplished. Richard Hargrave and Ann Hunnicutt to marry. Certificate for Thomas Nixon, son of Perce Nixon, dec'd., from monthly meeting near Simmons Creek in Pasquetank Co., NC.

22/5/1790. Stephen Peebles and Sarah Hollowell to marry.

19/6/1790. It appears that Richard Hargrave kept unseemly company with his now wife before the first meeting announcing their intentions which prevent their passing a second time.

17/7/1790. Marriage of Stephen Peebles orderly accomplished.

21/8/1790. Certificate from monthly meeting at the Western Branch for Robert Rickes, Junr. Reported by Stanton Meeting that James Jones, his wife Lucy Jones, Elizabeth Hicks and her dau. Fanny Hicks, request to be received into membership. Certificate for Elizabeth Hargrave, wife of Saml., from the monthly meeting at White Oak Swamp in Henrico Co.

18/9/1790. Samuel Butler and Ursly Ladd to marry.

20/11/1790. Elisha Johnson and Elizabeth Butler to marry. Marriage of Samuel Butler orderly accomplished.

18/12/1790. Elisha Johnson produced a certificate from monthly meeting at the Western Branch signifying his clearness in marriage.

15/1/1791. Marriage of Elisha Johnson orderly accomplished. Rebeca Davis disowned.

19/2/1791. Joel Judkins and Lucy Stanton to marry. Benjamin Russell informed this meeting that he was about to settle within the limits of Cedar Creek Monthly Meeting and requested a certificate for himself and daus. Sophia and Rebecah. Informed by Blackwater Meeting that Benjamin Bailey has lately had a bastard child sworn to him; has been in the practice of drinking to excess and swearing - disowned. Robert Hicks being removed and settled within Rich Square Monthly Meeting, Northampton Co., NC, requests a certificate.

19/3/1791. James Jones and wife received into membership. Certificate for Benja. Russell to be withheld until he settles debts.

18/5/1791. Marriage of Joel Judkins orderly accomplished. Peter Binford and Martha Brock to marry. Gravelly Run reports that Henry Sadler, his wife and family are removed and request certificate to Center Monthly Meeting in NC. Blackwater Meeting reports that Josiah Cook has a bastard child sworn to him. Certificate for Elizabeth Johnson late Butler from this meeting. Sarah Jordan disowned.

16/7/1791. The affairs of Benjamin Russell now settled, a certificate is produced for him and his two daus., Sophia and Rebecah, to Cedar Creek Monthly Meeting. William Hunnicutt and Ann Sears to marry. Marriage of Peter Binford orderly accomplished. Certificate for Henry Sadler, his wife Mary and their children, James, Zachariah, Eliza. Fanny, Mary and Sarah - directed to monthly meeting at Center in Guilford Co., NC. Burleigh Meeting reports that Jesse Hunnicutt has neglected attending meetings and frequents corrupting company and takes oaths.

17/9/1791. Anderson Simmons and Huldah Ladd to marry. John Cornwell, Junr., disowned. Certificate for Lucy Judkins, late Stanton, to monthly meeting at Rich Square in NC. Testification against Mary Bottom, late Hunnicutt. Charles Clary reinstated [now residing within the verge of the monthly meeting held at Wellses in Perguimons Co., NC]. Stanton Meeting reports that James Briggs has married contrary to Discipline - disowned.

15/10/1791. Marriage of William Hunnicutt orderly accomplished.

19/11/1791. Marriage of Anderson Simmons orderly accomplished.

17/12/1791. Samuel Hargrave, having removed and settled within the verge of White Oak Swam Monthly Meeting, requests a certificate.

18/2/1792. It appears that Robt. Bailey is in the practice of keeping bad company and much neglects the attendance of meetings [disowned]. John Bailey is married by the priest to his first cousin [Rebecca Bailey] - disowned. Certificate for Elizabeth Hargrave approved.

18/3/1792. Jesse Hair produced a certificate from monthly meeting at the Western Branch signifying his clearness of marriage engagements whereupon he and Sarah Harris published their intentions of marriage the second time. Jacob Ladd is removed and settled within the compass of Rich Square Monthly Meeting in NC and Saml. Bailey son of Edmond, is residing in within the compass of the Western Branch Monthly Meeting, and request certificates. Gravelly Run Meeting reports that Robert Langley has a number of Negroes under his care.

21/4/1792. Marriage of Jesse Hair is orderly accomplished. Ann C. Gorden disowned.

26/5/1792. Thomas Chappel and Jane Pretlow to marry.

21/7/1792. Thomas Hunnicutt and Mary Watkins to marry.

18/8/1792. Certificate for Wm. Wrenn and Lydia his wife from monthly meeting at Western Branch. A certificate for Sarah Hair, late Harriss, direct to monthly meeting at the Western Branch. Testification against Priscilla Murdock, late Binford, approved.

20/10/1792. Jesse Bailey requests a certificate signifying his clearness in marriage to monthly meeting at the Western Branch.

17/11/1792. Testification against Jane Hatch, late Hunnicutt.

19/1/1793. William Bott and Tabitha Sears to marry. Esther Durham to be received into membership. James Butler, senr., to move and settle in the limits of Souther River Monthly Meeting in Campbell Co.

16/2/1793. Benjamin Patterson and Patience Bailey to marry. Jeremiah Patterson and Faith Bailey to marry. Robert Ricks is moved within the limits of the Western Branch Monthly Meeting and requests a certificate. It appears that Amos Ladd of Mecklenburg Co. has married out of the unity of Friends [disowned].

15/3/1793. Marriage of Wm. Bott orderly accomplished. Benjamin Patterson and Jeremiah Patterson produced certificates from Rich Square Monthly Meeting signifying their clearness of marriage engagements. Certificate for James Butler, his wife Priscilla and their children, Mary, Tabitha, John, Ann, Sarah, Edward, Robert and Martha, to monthly meeting at South River. Certificate for Sarah Crew from White Oak Swamp Monthly Meeting in Henrico Co.

20/4/1793. Marriages of Benja. and Jeremiah Patterson orderly accomplished. James Stanton, son of Samson, is moved and settled in the verge of Rich Square Monthly Meeting and requests a certificate. Certificate for Pheruba Bailey from monthly meeting at the Western Branch. Patience and Faith Patterson (late Bailey) having removed and settled in the verge of Rich Square Monthly Meeting requests a certificate.

15/6/1793. John Heavernridge requests to be received into membership [Received and recommended to Gravelly Run].

20/7/1703. Certificates for Saml. Bailey, son of Edmd. and John Stanton, son of Jams(?), received from monthly meeting at the Wester Branch; also one for Wm. Cornwell from monthly meeting at Wellses in NC.

17/8/1793. Joseph Newby and Ann Davis to marry. Wm. Cornwell having returned to reside within the limits of the monthly meeting at Wellses in NC from which he came, a certificate is prepared.

21/9/1793. Joseph Newby produced a certificate from the monthly meeting at Wellses in Perquimons Co., NC, signifying his clearness in marriage.

19/10/1793. Marriage of Joseph Newby orderly accomplished. Certificate for Mary E. ...son from monthly meeting at the Wester Branch.

16/11/1793. John Heavenridge and wife [Margaret] request that their children be received into membership.

19/12/1793. Ann Newby, late Davis, being removed by marriage and settled within the limits of the monthly meeting of Wellses, NC; a certificate will be prepared.

15/2/1794. The following children of John Heavenridge will be received into membership: John, Isabel, Hannah, Margaret and William. Mary Butler having removed within the limits of Western Branch Monthly Meeting request certificate.

15/3/1794. Joseph Sebrell request to be received into membership. Blackwater Meeting reports that Lucy Clary has married a man contrary to the Discipline.

19/4/1794. Sarah Bailey, an Elder and member of Blackwater Meeting, d. 21/11/1793. Ruth Bailey, an Elder and member of the same meeting, d. 14/12/1793. Mary Pretlow, an Elder and member of said meeting, d. 9/12/1793. Paul Sears and Huldah Simmons to marry. Lucy Hart, late Clary, disowned. John White requests a certificate for his son Lemuel who is gone to reside in the verge of the Western Branch Monthly Meeting. Certificate for William Trotter from monthly meeting of the Western Branch. Burleigh Meeting reports that Jesse Hunnicutt has for some time past withdrawn himself from our religious meetings, frequents places of merry making, deviates from plainness, dances and has inlisted in the military service. Gravelly Run reports that Jane Evans requests to be received into membership [received]. Certificate for Ann Bailey from Western Branch Monthly Meeting.

24/5/1794. Gravelly Run Meeting reports that Jane Evans request to be received into membership.

21/6/1794. Marriage of Paul Sears orderly accomplished. Jess Hunnicutt disowned. Certificate for James Stanton, son of Samson, from monthly meeting at Jack Swamp in NC.

19/7/1794. Stanton Meeting reports that Susannah Tharp had removed and settled within the limits of the Western Branch Monthly Meeting.

12/8/1794. Certificate for Susannah Thorp to monthly meeting at the Western Branch. Stanton Meeting is satisfied to receive the children of Richard Wrenn and his wife, namely, daus. Lukey (Looky) and Salley; the eldest requests for herself. John Hamlin requests a certificate for purposes of marriage to monthly meeting at the Western Branch.

20/9/1794. Samuel Hunnicutt and Pheraby Brock to marry.

15/11/1794. Marriage of Samuel Hunnicutt orderly accomplished. Blackwater Meeting reports that James Butler, son of James, is about to remove within the verge of South River Monthly Meeting and requests a certificate.

20/12/1794. Stanton Meeting reports that Meriam Hargrave has married a man contrary to Discipline. Reported that Jane Bailey has for a considerable time conducted herself very disorderly and continues to hold a slave [disowned]. Certificate for Mary Horsefall and son from Bridge ... Monthly Meeting

17/1/1795. Stanton Meeting reports that James Bailey, son of Mich., has absented himself from our religious meetings, deviated from plainness in speech and apparel, dances and frequents places of merriment [disowned]. Certificate from Brighouse Monthly Meeting in England for Mary Horsfall and Edmond Horsfall, her son about 14 years old, was received, they some time past resided within the limits of this meeting, but being informed the said Mary Horsfall is removed to New York. Miriam Hancock, late Hargrave, disowned. A complaint against Elizabeth Hargrave for holding slaves.

21/3/1795. Gravelly Run Meeting reports that John Crew and family [wife: Judith, children: Charles, Martha, Caleb, Sarah, Anna, Joshua, John and Elizabeth] are about to remove and settle within the limits of Westhill Monthly Meeting (Surry Co.) in NC and requests a certificate. It appears that John Ladd, Junr. has for sometime past neglected the attendance of our religious meetings, deviated from plainness in speech and apparel and is in the practice of overseeing slaves. Stanton Meeting reports that Richard Hargrave has absented himself from religious meeting and is guilty of gaming despite repeated visits with him. Certificate for John Bailey, son of Armiger, from monthly meeting at the Western Branch.

18/4/1795. Certificate for Hannah Crew from White Oak Swamp Monthly Meeting. Blackwater Monthly Meeting reports that Mary Hargrave,

widow of Silas, has conducted herself very disorderly [disowned].
[... missing men's minutes 5th month 1795 through 1st month 1796.]

20/6/1795. Blackwater Meeting reports that Martha Bailey has married a man contrary to Discipline.

18/7/1795. Martha Rowe, late Bailey, disowned. Certificate for Elizabeth Hamlin, wife of John, from the Western Branch Monthly Meeting dated 23/5/1795. William Hollowell and Susanna Peebles to marry.

15/8/1795. Lemuel Ely and Jane Chappel to marry. Abidan Bailey and Elizabeth Briggs to marry. Certificate for Mary Butler from Western Branch Monthly Meeting.

19/9/1795. Marriage of William Hollowell orderly accomplished.

18/10/1795. Marriage of Lemuel Ely orderly accomplished. Marriage of Abidan Bailey orderly accomplished. James Ladd and Jane Evans to marry.

21/11/1795. Marriage of Jane Evans orderly accomplished.

19/12/1795. Daniel Butler and Sarah Watkins to marry. Informed that Stephen Butler and family about to remove within the limits of South River Monthly Meeting; certificate prepared.

16/1/1796, Jane Ladd, late Evans, being removed and settled within the verge of White Oak Swamp Monthly Meeting, requests a certificate.

20/2/1796. Daniel Butler and Sarah Watkins have declined their intentions of marriage for the present. Benjamin Pritlow and Samuel Bailey, Jr. disowned. Stephen Butler's affairs are now settled. Certificate for Samuel Bailey, son of Edmond. Children of John Butler to be received: Stanton, Elizabeth and John.

19/3/1796. James Hunnicutt and Delitha Bailey to marry. Certificate for Jane Ladd to monthly meeting at White Oak Swamp.

16/4/1796. Robert Hunnicutt, an Elder and member of Burleigh Meeting, d. 28/4/1795. Marriage of Daniel Butler orderly accomplished. Stanton Meeting reports that Banester Betts has neglected attendance of our religious meetings, deviates from plainness of speech and is guilty of using profane language [disowned].

28/5/1796. Marriage of James Hunnicutt orderly accomplished.

17/9/1796. Gravelly Run Meeting reports that Robert Evans, Junr. request to be received into membership [received].

15/10/1796. Burleigh Meeting reports that Hannah Crew has married a man contrary to Discipline - disowned.

19/11/1796. Testification against Hannah Hunnicutt, late Crow [disowned].

17/12/1796. Mary Horsefall has settled quite remote from Friends and requests that her certificate remain with this meeting. It appears that

Mary Clary has married a man contrary to Discipline.

21/1/1797. Stanton Meeting reports that Hamlin Hargrave is guilty of drinking to excess, keeping bad company and using profane language [disowned]. Sarah Hart, late Cary, disowned. It appears that James Butler has married contrary to the rules of our Society - disowned. Certificate from White Oak Swamp Monthly Meeting for Rebecca Johnson and her three children: Nancy, Elizabeth and Benjamin.

18/3/1797. William Hunnicutt, Junr., has removed within the limits of South River Monthly Meeting and requests a certificate. Peggy Warren has married a man contrary to Discipline - disowned.

15/4/1797. Samuel Bailey, an Elder and member of Blackwater Meeting, d. 27/6/1796. Margaret Spratly, late Warrin, disowned.

19/5/1797. Exum Bailey being removed within the limits of the Western Branch Monthly Meeting, requests a certificate.

17/6/1797. Certificate for Sarah Ladd [women's minutes gives name as Sarah Sadler] to monthly meeting at Jack Swamp in NC. Ann Dilworth has requested to be received into membership.

16/9/1797. Zachariah Bailey and Mary White to marry. William Butler and Mary Butler to marry. Sarah and Prisillah Hunnicutt have neglected attendance of our meetings and connected with disorderly practices [disowned].

21/10/1797. John Stanton and Lydia Butler to marry.

18/11/1797. Marriage of Zachariah Bailey orderly accomplished. Marriage of Wm. Butler orderly accomplished. John Heavenridge and family have removed and settled in the limits of New Hope Monthly Meeting in Tennessee.

16/12/1797. Sarah and Precila Hunnicutt disowned. Thomas Clary and Mary Bailey to marry. Marriage of John Stanton orderly accomplished. Certificate for John Heavenridge, his wife Margaret, and children: John, Isabella, Hannah, Margaret, William and Nathaniel - to New Hope Monthly Meeting, Washington Co., TN.

20/1/1798. Stanton Meeting reports that Mathew Bailey has used criminal conversation with a young woman and has married contrary to the rules of our Society and has absented himself from our religious meetings [disowned].

17/3/1798. Marriage of Thomas Clary orderly accomplished. Samuel Binford and Mary Hunnicutt to marry. Certificate for Martha Butler to monthly meeting at Western Branch. Blackwater Meeting reports Josiah Davice has married contrary to Discipline [disowned].

21/4/1798. Rebeckah Sebrel request to be received into membership. William Trotter being returned within the limits of the Western

Branch Monthly Meeting requests a certificate. Rebecah Sebrell requests to be received into membership. Blackwater Meeting reports that Elizabeth Bailey has conducted herself very disorderly and has neglected attending meetings and continues to hold a slave [disowned].

26/5/1798. Marriage of Samuel Binford orderly accomplished. Blackwater Monthly Meeting reports that Lemuel White has removed and settled within the limits of Western Branch Monthly Meeting.

16/6/1798. Lidia Cook [wife of Josiah Cook] requests that her two youngest children, Mary and Wm. Cook (who have not a birthright with us) may be received into membership. Joseph Sebrel and wife request that their children [Benjamin, Matthew, Josiah, Sally and Susan] be received into membership [received].

21/7/1798. Testification against Elizabeth Bailey. Certificates received for Jacob Ladd, his wife Elizabeth and son Jeremiah, from monthly meeting at Jack Swamp, Northampton Co., NC dated 2/6/1798.

18/8/1798. Ursuly Bailey disowned [neglecting meetings deviating from plainness and marrying a man not of our Society].

15/9/1798. Edmond Bailey and Huldah Simmons to marry.

20/10/1798. Thomas Hunnicutt and Elizabeth Peebles to marry.

17/11/1798. Marriage of Edmond Bailey orderly accomplished.

15/12/1798. Marriage of Thomas Hunnicutt orderly accomplished. Lemuel Johnson and Elizabeth Hunnicutt to marry.

19/1/1799. Lemual Johnson produced a certificate from monthly meeting at the Western Branch signifying his clearness in marriage. Blackwater Meeting reports that John Pinner has been in the practice of gaming and has absconded to defraud his creditors [disowned].

16/2/1799. Marriage of Lemuel Johnson orderly accomplished.

16/3/1799. Benjamin Ladd and Sarah Binford to marry. Elizabeth Johnston, late Hunnicutt being removed to settle within the limits of the Western Branch requests certificate.

20/4/1799. Blackwater and Stanton to constitute one monthly meeting and Burleigh and Gravelly Run the other. Benjamin Ladd produced a certificate from monthly meeting at White Oak Swamp in Henrico Co. Certificate for Elizabeth Johnson, late Hunnicutt to monthly meeting at the Western Branch.

17/5/1799. Marriage of Benjamin Ladd orderly accomplished. Micajah Bailey and James Bailey are now removing within the limits of the Western Branch Monthly Meeting; certificates will be prepared.

15/6/1799. Burleigh Meeting reports that William Hollowell has a claim of debt against Stephen Peebles and suffers a loss by delay in payment.

[men's minutes missing 17/8/1799 through 1800 - only women's minutes from here on ...]

19/8/1799. Sarah Ladd, late Binford, having removed and settled within the verge of White Oak Swamp Monthly Meeting, requests certificate.

16/11/1799. Certificate from Jack Swamp Monthly Meeting for Agathy El..y and her two daus., Kezier and Caster.

18/1/1800. Sarah Elison, a member of Blackwater Meeting has conducted herself disorderly and countenances loose company at her house and behaves basely.

15/3/1800. Joseph Patterson and Mary Bailey to marry. William Trotter and Penninah Bailey to marry.

24/5/1800. Marriage of Joseph Patterson orderly accomplished. Marriage of William Trotter orderly accomplished. Informed that Elizabeth Davis has been so imprudent as to forsake her mother's house and take up with a man of colour [disowned]. Certificate from Western Branch Monthly Meeting for Ann Bailey and her dau. Mary.

24/5/1800. Mary Patterson, late Bailey, being removed and settled in the limits of Jack Swamp Monthly Meeting, requests a certificate.

19/7/1800. Informed that Ann Hall, late Bailey, and Mary Johnston, late Bailey, have married contrary to Discipline - disowned.

16/8/1800. Ruth Bailey having removed within the limits of Jack Swamp Monthly Meeting, requests a certificate. Penninah Trotter, late Bailey, having removed and settled in the limits of the Western Branch Monthly Meeting, requests a certificate.

19/9/1800. John Butler and Mary Harris to marry. Judith Ladd continues to conduct herself very disorderly - disowned.

15/11/1800. Marriage of John Buttler and Mary Harris orderly accomplished.

Marriages

Joshua Moore of Perquimons Co., NC and Hannah Hargrave, dau. of Joseph Hargrave of Surry Co., VA, 23/3/1760.

James Bates of York Co., VA and Elizabeth Hunnicut, dau. of John Hunnicut, dec'd., of Prince George Co., 3/11/1762.

Robert Wyke Hunnicutt, son of Robert Hunnicutt of Prince George Co. and Priscilla Binford, dau. of Peter Binford of same county, 22/2/1764.

John Sears, son of John Sears, son of Paul Sears of Dinwiddie Co. and Sarah Peebles, dau. of Peter Peebles of Prince George Co., with consent of parents, 24/2/1768.

Wyke Hunnicut, son of Wyke Hunnicutt late of Prince George Co. and Ann Bailey, dau. of Anselm Bailey of Surry Co., with consent of parents, 18/6/1769.

Robert Hunnicutt, son of Wyke Hunnicutt, dec'd., and Priscilla Hunnicutt, widow of Robert Wyke Hunnicutt, both of Prince George Co., at Burleigh, 16/7/1769.

Samuel Bailey, son of Anselm Bailey, Junr. of Surry Co., and Sarah Hunnicutt, dau. of Wyke Hunnicutt of same county, 21/1/1753.

William Binford of Prince George Co. and Mary Peebles of the same county, 18/7/1756.

David Davis of Southampton Co. and Lydia Kitchen, 19/12/1756.

James Ladd, son of James Ladd of Charles City Co., and Sarah Binford, dau. of Peter Binford of Prince George Co., 24/5/1761 at Burleigh.

John Fowler, son of Godfree Fowler, dec'd., of Chesterfield Co. and Eliza. Sears, dau. of Paul Sears of Dinwiddie Co., 3/11/1762.

William Hunnicutt, son of Peter Hunnicutt of Prince George Co. and Mary Butler, dau. of James Butler of Dinwiddie Co., with consent of parents, 21/4/1762.

Benjamin Crews, son of Andrew Crews of Charles City Co. and Margret Hunnicutt, dau. of Robert Hunnicutt of Prince George Co., with consent of parents, 21/3/1767.

James Clary of Southampton Co. and Martha Stevenson, dau. of Peter Stevenson of the same county, 21/7/1760.

Edmond Bailey, son of Benjamin Bailey of Southampton Co. and Eliza Womble of the same county, 19/9/1762.

Jerimiah Reams, son of William Reams of Dinwiddie Co. and Margaret Merrymoon, dau. of John Merrymoon, 25/2/1768 at a publick meeting at the house of Benjamin Pattison in Amelia Co.

David Merrymoon, son of John and Hannah Merrymoon of Amelia Co. and Elizabeth Pattison of the same county, 5/2/1768.

John Pleasants of Henrico Co. and Meriam Hunnicutt of Prince George Co., 21/10/1769 at Black Water.

James Hunnicut, son of John Hunnicutt, dec'd., of Prince George Co. and Rebeckah Pretlow, dau. of Joshua Pretlow, dec'd., late of Sussex Co., 17/5/1772.

James Brock of Sussex Co. and Sarah Bailey, dau. of Benja. Bailey of Southampton Co., 18/10/1772.

John Smith of Southampton Co. and Martha Bailey, dau. of Benja. Bailey of the same county, 18/10/1772.

John White of Sussex Co. and Ann Cornwell, dau. of Samuel Cornwell, dec'd., of the same county, 22/2/1775.

Matthew Harris of Isle of Wight Co. and Mary House of Southampton Co., 22/2/1775.

Chappel Binford, son of Peter Binford of Prince George Co. and Martha Hunnicutt, dau. of Robt. and Ann Hunnicutt of the same county, with consent of parents, 21/6/1775.

David Fisher of Dinwiddie Co., coachmaker and Martha Butler, dau. of William Butler and Elisabeth Butler of the same county, 23/3/1775.

Benjamin Johnson, son of David and Mary Johnson of Hanover Co. and Rebecca Pretlow, dau. of Samuel and Mary Pretlow, 13/11/1775.

William Ladd, son of James Ladd of Charles City Co., dec'd., and Mary Hunnicutt, dau. of Robt. Hunnicutt of Prince George Co., with consent of parents, 20/6/177-.

James Watkins of Sussex Co. and Ann White of the same county, 10/11/1770.

James Binford, son of Peter Binford and Elizabeth, dau. of Anderson Simmons, both of Prince George Co. [... rest of page missing. See minutes.]

William Butler of Dinwiddie Co. and Faith Stanton of Southampton Co., 22/8/1779 in Sussex Co.

Josiah Jordan, Junr. of Southampton Co., son of Matthias Jordan, late of Parqustank Co., NC, dec'd., and Sarah Hunnicutt, dau. of Glaister Hunnicutt of Sussex Co., VA, 18/9/1780.

Samuel Cornwell, son of Sam. Cornwell, dec'd., of Sussex Co., and Sarah Bailey, dau. of Saml. Bailey of Surry Co., 22/4/1781 at Blackwater Meeting in Surry Co.

Thomas Walthall of Chesterfield Co. and Elizabeth Bott, dau. of Wm. Bott of Amelia Co., 31/3/1779, at their meeting in Amelia Co. near Deep Creek.

Thomas Pretlow, son of Joshua Pretlow, dec'd., of Sussex Co. and Ann Bailey, dau. of Saml. Bailey and his wife Sarah of Surry Co., 20/8/1783 at the meeting house in Surry Co.

Thomas Walthall of Dinwiddie Co. and Susanna Peebles of Prince George Co., with consent of parents, 24/8/1785, at Burleigh Meeting House.

John Andrews of Dinwiddie Co. and Sarah Butler, dau. of Joseph and Miriam Butler of same county, 15/2/1786 at Gravelly Run Meeting.

James D. Ladd, son of James Ladd of Charles City Co. and Jane Evans, dau. of Robt. Evans of the town of Petersburg in VA, with consent of parents, 20/10/1795 at Gravelly Run Meeting.

Manumissions

John Cornwell of Sussex Co. manumits Negro man Cuffey, age about 22, 14/11/1776.

Robert Hunnicutt, son of Peter, of Prince George Co. manumits Hannah, age about 46, Negro man Jemmy age about 33, Negro girl Judy age about 20. 18/11/1776.

Robert Hunnicutt of Prince George Co. manumits a Negro boy named Ned, age about 20, at age 21 which will be on 17/11/1777; also a Negro boy named Dick age about 15, at age 21 which will be on 25/3/1782; also Negro boy named Isaac age about 15, at age 21 which will be on 26/4/1782; also Negro boy named John age about 2, at age 21 which will be on 25/4/1795. Signed 18/11/1776.

Robert Hunnicutt, son of Peter of Prince George Co., manumits Negro boy Davie age about 12, at age 21 which will be on 13/6/1786. Signed 24/12/1776.

James Watkins of Sussex Co. manumits Negro boy named Kinchin age about 20, at age 21 which will be on 25/12/1777. Signed 21/12/1776.

Sampson Stanton of Southampton Co. manumits Negro boy named Jim age about 14, at age 21 which will be on 1/9/1783; also Negro man named Sam Senr, age about 60; Negro woman named Nanny age about 26; Negro girl named Lucy age about 11, at age 18 which will be on 18/12/1783; also Negro girl named Siar age about 8, at age 18 which will be on 7/4/1786; Negro boy named Tom age about 6, at age 21 which will be on 3/8/1791; also Negro boy named Sam age about 3, at age 21 which will be 15/1/1794; also Negro boy named Moses age about one, at age 21 which will be on 1/8/1796. Signed 20/11/1776.

John White of Sussex Co. manumits Negro woman named Beck age about 40; also Negro boy named Bob age about 15; also Negro boy named Roger age about 8, at age 21 which will be on 1/12/1789; also Negro boy named Lewis age about 5 at age, at age 21 which will be on 1/11/1792. 20/11/1776.

Mary Hargrave of Surry Co., widow of Joseph Hargrave, Junr., whose will was dated 10 Aug 1775, manumits three Negroes: Sam age 60; Cupid age about 40; Lucy age about 25. 21/12/1776.

John Hunnicutt of Prince George Co. manumits Negro woman named Cate age about 23. 24/12/1776.

Thomas Hunnicutt of Prince George Co. manumits Negro man named Joe age about 22; also Negro man named Nathan age about 21. 24/12/1776.

William Hunnicutt of Prince George Co. manumits Negro woman named Phebe age about 32; also Negro girl Aggey age about 14, at age 18 which will be on 8/1/1781; also Negro girl Grace age about 12, at age 18 which will be on 8/1/1783. 8/1/1777.

Sarah Hunnicutt of Prince George Co. manumits 6 Negroes above the age of 21: Peter, Tom, Joan, Fortune, Lyddy and Milly; also 7 Negroes under the age of 21: James, Ben, Sam, Peter, Janny, Annaky and Hannah, at age 18 for the females and at age 21 for the males. 15/3/1777.

Wyke Hunnicutt of Prince George Co. manumits Negro woman named Bett age about 45; also Negro girl named Amy age about 13, at age 18 which will be on 25/9/1781; also Negro woman named Silla age about 22; also Negro man named Jesse age about 25; Negro boy named Moses age about 20, at age 21 which will be on 20/7/1777; Negro boy named Gaberal age about 20, at age 21 which will be on 15/6/1777; Negro named Duke age about 20, at age 21 which will be on 13/3/1778; Negro woman Milly age about 20. 8/2/1777 and 15/3/1777.

William Simmons of Prince George Co. manumits Negro woman named Aggey age about 57; also Negro man named Linn age about 21; also Negro girl named Dol age about 10, a⁺ age 18 which will be on 15/7/1785. 10/1/1778.

John Butler, son of Wm., of Dinwiddie Co. manumits Negro man named Dick age about 43; also Negro boy named Sam, age 18, at age 21 which will be on 31/12/1781; Negro woman named Amy, age about 20. 18/2/1779.

James Butler, Junr., of Dinwiddie Co. manumits Negro woman named Judy age about 50; also Negro boy named Jimmy age about 14, at age 21 which will be on 31/10/1785; also Negro boy named Dick age about 11, at age 21 which will be on 11/1/1789. 27/5/1779.

William Butler of Dinwiddie Co. manumits Negro man named Will age about 65; Negro man named Toney age about 58; Negro woman Fillis age about 31; also Negro man named Nedd age about 27; also Negro man Dick age about 29; also Negro woman named Jenny age about 22; also Negro man named Jemmy age about 20, after 31/12/1780; Negro boy named Sam age about 11, at age 21 which will be on 11/7/1789; also Negro boy named Abraham age about 8, at age 21 which will be on 9/7/1792. 31/5/1779.

CHUCKATUCK MONTHLY MEETING

Minutes and Register

Marriage of Edmond Belson of Nansemond County and Mary Crewe of Isle of Wight County, 13/10/1684. Mother: Elizabeth Belson, Mary Tooke, 13/10/1684.

Marriage of John Scott and Elizabeth Belson of Nansemond County, 19/8/1682. Father: William Scott; Mother: Elizabeth Belson; Her brother: Edmond Belson. His brother: William Scott, Jr.

Children of Edmond Belson and Elizabeth his wife of Nansemond County: Edmond b. 11/9/1664; Elizabeth b. last day of sixth month 1666. Mary b. 24/3/1673.

Marriage of James Jordan of Nansemond County and Elizabeth Ratliff of Isle of Wight County, ∠9/3/1688. Father: Thomas Jordan, Richard Ratliff; Mother: Margaret Jordan; Cousin: Thomas Davis, John Neuell.

Children of James Jordan and Elizabeth his wife: Elizabeth, ?; James, ?

Elizabeth Jordan, wife of James Jordan, d. last of the sixth month, 1695.

Leaven Bufkin and Dorrithy Newby of Nansemond, 17/2/1688. Father: William Newby.

Children of Leaven Bufkin and Dorrithy his wife: Leaven, b. 9/12/1688.

Priests tithes seized from Joshua Jordan, Jan. 29, 1717 and May 22, 1715.

Children of Thomas Jordan and Margrett his wife: Thomas Jordan, b. 6/1/1660; John, b. 17/6/1663; James, b. 23/11/1665; Robart, b. 11/7/1668; Richard, b. 6/6/1670; Joseph, b. 8/7/1672; Benjamin, b. 18/7/1674; Mathew, b. 1/11/1676; Samuel, b. 15/2/1679; Joshua, b. last day of 6th month 1681.

Thomas Jordan of Chuckatuck in Nansemond County b. 1634 and in 1660 joined the Society of Friends; d. 8/10/1699 about 2 p.m. Sarah Jordan, great grandchild of above Elder Tho. Jordan, and dau. of Jos. and Anne Jordan, b. 12/2/1731. Abigail Jordan, dau. of Joseph and Anne Jordan, b. 14/7/1733. Margarett Jordan, 3rd and last dau. of sd. Joseph and Anne ---.

Formerly of Nansemond Co.: Tho: Page & Alce his wife: Tho: Page, b. 7/2/1680; Rebecka, b. 8/11/1682.

Marriage of Henry Wiggs and Katheren Garrett, 3/12/1674, at Chuckatuck.

Of Isle of Wight Co.: Children of Henry Wiggs and Katheren his first wife: Henry Wiggs, b. 6/11/1675. Children of Henry Wiggs and Katheren his second wife: Cathren, b. 2/8/1681; Mary, b. 2nd month 1687; Elizabeth, b. 16/12/1689; Sara, b. 19/12/1693; William, b. last of

5th month 1696.
Of Isle of Wight Co.: Children of John Harris and Margret: Margarett Harris, b. 13/6/1682; Allis, b. 7/6/1685. Children of John and Elizabeth his second wife: Elizabeth, b. 15/3/1692; Isabella, b. 7/4/1695; Sasanna, b. 19/11/1699; Ann, b. 18/11/1702; Mary, b. 12/3/1706. Margret, first wife of John Harris d. 16/11/1687.

Children of Thomas Jordan the younger and his wife Elizabeth (recorded in Chuckatuck): Thomas, b. 10/1/1681; Elizabeth, b. 18/9/1683; Martha, b. 22/11/1685; William, b. 25/5/1688

Children of William Scott and Elizabeth his wife: Elizabeth, b. 12 Dec 1675; William, b. 27/Dec 1678; John, b. 3/2/1682; Robt., b. 19/4/1685; Sarah Scot, b. 5/3/1694; Kathren, b. 9/4/1697.

Children of John Scott and his wife Elizabeth: William, b. 8/3/1683; Elizabeth, b. 5/2/1686.

Children of Edmond Belson and Mary his wife: Mary b. 24/11/1685; Elizabeth b. 13/11/1687.

Children of Benjamin Small and Elizabeth his wife: Mary b. 30/1/1702; Hannah b. last day of the third month 1704; Amy b. 22/1/170?

Marriage of John Morry and Elizabeth Yarrett, dau. of William Yarrett of Isle of Wight County, 22/6/1678.

Marriage of William Oudelant of Nansemond County, and Christian Taberer, dau. of Thomas Taberer of Isle of Wight Co., at the house of Elizabeth Oudelants his mother, 15/9/1678.

Children of William Oudelant and Christian his wife: Cornelius b. 8/5/1681; William b. 6/11/1682; Thomas b. 19/12/1684.

Marriage of Thomas Jordan, son of Thomas Jordan of Chuckatuck, Nansemond County, and Elizabeth Burgh, dau. of William Burgh, dec'd., 6/10/1679. His mother: Margarett Jordan. Her brother: Georg: Billingsly. His 3 brothers: John, James and Robart Jordan. Her sister: Mourrning Burgh.

Children of Isaac Rickesis and Kathren his wife: Isaac, b. 17/6/1669; Wm., b. 5/8/1670; Jno., b. 30/10/1672; Abraham, b. 3/10/1674; Jacob, b. 17/1/1677; Robert, b. 14/10/1679; Benjamin, b. 17/11/1682; Kathren, b. 20th day of 10th month and lived 10 months and died in 1684; Richard, b. 30/5/1685; Jeane, b. last day of 6th month 1687; James, b. 17/1/1690.

Children of James Denson and Sarah his wife: Frances (dau.), b. 3/11/1708.

Marriage of Hugh Bressie and Sara Campion of Isle of Wight County, 14/3/1680 at the house of his uncle, William Bressie.

Marriage of Henry Hollowell, son of Tho: Hollowell of Elizabeth River and

Elizabeth Cotching, dau. of Thomas Cotching of Chuckatuck, dec'd., 7/8/1680. Mother: Alce Hollowell. 2 Brothers: Tho: Hollowelll, Junr., Phil Howerd. Sisters: Sara Howard, Sara Hollowell, Christian Oudelant.

William Sanders and Mary Hall of Nansemond, 9/4/1682.

Tho. Duke of Nansemond Co. has married one not of our Society by a hireling priest. 8/3/1701.

Letter from England searching for Christopher Ouldfeild as he left his wife.

Testimony by Edward Perkins against the preaching of John Parrott, 3/12/1678.

Marriage of John Jordan, son of Thomas Jordan of Chuckatuck, Nansemond Co., and Margret Burgh of the same place, at his father's house, 9/12/1688. Father: Tho: Jordan. Mother: Margaret Jordan. Uncle: John Brassere. Brothers: Tho. Jordan, Junr., Robard Jordan.

Marriage of Robart Jordan of Nansemond Co. and Christian Oudeland of Isle of Wight County, 9/12/1687. Father: Tho: Jordan, Thomas Taberer. Mother: Margaret Jordan. Uncle: John Brasseres, James Davis. Brothers: Thomas Jordan, Junr., John Jordan. Aunt: Abagall Brasser, Margaret Davis. Sister: Elizabeth Jordan, Christian Jordan.

Christian, dau. Robert and Christian Jordan, b. 23/1/1689; d. 26/6/1689.

Children of Thos. Trotter and Anne his wife: Thos. and Joseph, twins, b. 14/6/1738; Joseph d. 6/4/1739 and his brother Thos. Trotter d. 6/7/1739; Thos. b. 25/2/17--; Anne, b. 5/6/--; Elizabeth, b. 9/12/1748. Anne Trotter d. 20/1/1754, being in 45 years of her age, a minister 16 years.

Children of Thomas Hollowell of Elizabeth River and his wife Alice: Sarah, b. 1/11/1647; Thomas, b. 22/1/1649; Henry, b. 18/8/1652; John, b. 22/4/1655, d. 10/3/1671; Joseph, b. 15/6/1657; Benjamine, b. 28/12/1659; Elizabeth, b. 9/7/1662; Alice, b. 16/12/1664; Edmond, b. 15/9/1667; John, b. 5/9/1672.

Children of William Yarrett and Margrett his wife: Katheren, b. 1/3/1651; William, b. 5/9/1656; Elizabeth, b. 15/3/1658; Margrett, b. 1st day of last month 1664.

Children of Margrett Tabberer wife to Thomas Tabbarer of the Isle of Wight County: Elizabeth Wood, born to Margrett's first husband, John Wood, 27/7/1656; Christian Tabbarer, dau. of Margaret and Thomas Tabbarer her second husband, b. 9th month 1661; Elizabeth Tabberer, dau. of Margaret and Thomas Tabberer, b. last of the 10th month 1663.

Children of Robt. Jordan and Mary his wife: Thomas b.13/4/1693; Mary

b. 18/4/1691; Robert, b. 27/10/1692; Joseph, b. 18/9/1695; Mary, 24/12/1699; Margrett, b. 12/2/1702; Elizabeth, b. 17/12/1705; Edmond and Bellsen (twins) b. 17/6/1707; Bellsen d. 9/10/1707. Samuel, b. 29/4/1711.

Children of William Scott and Christian his wife: Mary, b. 4/7/1708; Christian Scott the wife of William Scott and Daughter of Robert Jordan by his first wife d. 12/7/1708.

Marriage of John Murrey and Elizabeth Hitchins of the Isle of Wight County, 15/2/1686.

Children of Joseph Jordan (minister) and his wife Ann: Sarah, b. 12/2/1731 (10 a.m.); Abigal, b. 19/7/1733 (12 a.m.); Margreat, b. 29/10/1736 (died in infancy); Joseph Jordan d. 19/10/1736.

Thomas Hollowell and his wife Alice testify that their children are unlawfully married by a priest.

William _____ testifies to the character of John Perrott and his being taken prisoner by Isle of Wight County sheriff and the imprisonment of John Browne.

Confession of Thomas Thurston of having touched Sara Fuller of Maryland, "and whatsoever may justly be layed unto my charge," First month of 1675.

It was decided that Richard Basnett may be allowed to accept a court position which does not require him to take an oath; 17/9/1677.

Marriage of John Collings and Mary Foake of Surry County, at her father's house, 14/12/1682. Father: John Barnes.

Marriage of Robart Jones and Martha Rice of Nansemond County, at his home, 10/5/1683.

Marriage of John Benson and Mary Bridell of Isle of Wight County, 12/9/1692. Mother: Francis Bridell; Mother: Francis Benson.

Marriage of Joseph Merrideth and Sara Benson of Nansemond County, 11/4/1696. Father: Samson Merrideth Mother: Frances Benson of Isle of Wight County.

Marriage of Benjamin Small and Elizabeth Hollowell of Nansemond County, 12/1/1699.

Marriage of Joseph Kenerly of Dorchester County and Sara Ratliff, 20/7/1696. Father: Richard Ratliff of Isle of Wight County.

Marriage of Edmond Belson of Nansemond County and Joan Ridick, 11/5/1689. Father: Robart Ridick.

Marriage of Thomas Newman and Mary Ratliff of Isle of Wight County, 13/2/1699.

Marriage of Mathew Jordan and Dorrithy Bufkin of Nansemond County, 6/7/1699. Father: Thomas Jordan of Chuckatuck.

Marriage of Jacob Rickesis and Mary Exum of Isle of Wight County, 14/10/1699. Father:Isaac Rickesis.

Marriage of Thomas Gay and Rebecca Page of the Isle of Wight County, 11/11/1699. Father: Thomas Page.

Marriage of William Powel and Mary Page of Isle of Wight County, 14/2/1700. Mother Elizabeth Powel; Father: Thomas Page.

Marriage of Richard Rattcliff and Elizabeth Hollowell of the Isle of Wight County, 18/7/1700. Father: Richard Ratcliff, Sr.; Mother: Elizabeth Rattclift; Sister: Rebecca Ratclift.

Children of Richard Ratliff of Chuckatuck: Elizabeth, b. 21/7/1668; Sarah b. 19/9/1670; Richard b. 13/7/1672; Cornelius 15/1/1674(or 1745); Mary b. 5/2/1679; John b. 20/2/1681; Rebecca b. 3/5/1684.

Children of Thomas Duke: Thomas b. 7/6/1671; Mary b. 10/10/1674.

Marriage of James Jordwin and Jane Roseter of Elizabeth River, 14/7/1701.

Marriage of Thomas Page of western branch of Isle of Wight County and Isabell Lawrence of western branch of Nansemond County, 15/1/1702. Father: Thomas Page; Mother: Alice Page; Father Henry Lawrence; Brothers: Michall Lawrence, Thomas Lawrence.

Children of Thomas Page and Alice his wife: Thomas b. 11/2/1680; Rebecka b. 8/11/1682.

Marriage of Mathew Jordan of Nansemond County and Susanna Brosy of Isle of Wight County, 17/3/1702.

Marriage of Abraham Rickesis and Mary Bellson of the western branch of Nansemond County, 16/3/1703; Father: Isaac Rickesis; Father: Edmond Bellson; Mother: Kathren Rickesis; Brother: John Rickesis, Robert Rickesis, Jacob Rickesis; Uncle: William Scot, Benjamin Small; Aunt: Elizabeth Small, Mary Jordan.

Marriage of George Murrell of Surry County and Mary Waters of Isle of Wight County, 16/2/1704. Father: George Murrell, Walter Waters; Mother: Elizabeth Murrell.

Debts to the widow of Jacob Rickes, Mary Rickes, paid by Isaac Rickes, Jr. and Robart Rickes sons of Isaac Rickes, Sr., settling differences between Jeremiah Exum and Isaac Rickes, Sr., 8/1/1703.

Marriage of Francis Braise and Elizabeth Wiggs of Isle of Wight County, 15/7/1713. Father: Huge Braise, Henry Wiggs (deceased).

Marriage of Cornelius Ratcliff and Elizabeth Jordan of Isle of Wight County, 23/9/1721.

William Dawson and Amey Small, 20/12/1723.

Marriage of Thomas White and Rachel Jordan of Isle of Wight County, 13/7/1719. Father: John White, Joshua Jordan.

Marriage of John Page of Isle of Wight County and Felicia Hall of Nansemond County, No date. Father: Moses Hall.

Marriage of Joseph Jordan of North Carolina and Mary Rix of Isle of Wight County, 10/2/1723. Father: Joseph Jordan, Abraham Rix.

Marriage of William Wilkinson of Nansemond County and Rebeca Powel of Isle of Wight County, 21/9/1723 Father: Henry Wilkinson, William Powel.

Marriage of Joseph Small and Ann Owen of Nansemond County, 18/10/1722. Father: John Small, Gilbert Owen.

Marriage of William Bogue of North Carolina and Sarah Duke of Nansemond County, 15/12/1728. Father Thomas Duke.

Benjamin Chapman testifies to having taken Mary Copland to wife "contrary to the order of truth" 12/3/1703.

Apology by Thomas Page, admitting to subscribing to Thomas Sikes certificate of marriage, 9/10/1705.

Land dispute between Daniel Sanbourn and Richard Rattclift arbitrated by John Richardson and Edward Thomas, 6/1/1702.

Henry Hacklet disowned by meeting, 12/6/1702

Consent given to Moses Hall to marry Margrett Duke by Thomas Duke, Sr., 7/11/1707.

Inventory of William Brosy's estate, 1701.

Marriage of John Scot and Joan Fook of Isle of Wight County. Father: William Scot, Thomas Fook. Came before meeting to be married, but as Joan Fook was not of the faith the marriage was not approved and John Scot is struck from the society, 13/4/1706.

Testimony by John Harris apologizing for signing the marriage certificate of John Scot and Joan Fook, 12/7/1706.

Testimony by William Scot against the marriage of his son John Scot with Joan Fook, 12/7/1706.

Testimony by John Rattliff apologizing for attending William Oadelants marriage.

Testimony by Francis B. Briddell apologizing for having been a witness to Thomas Sikes marriage.

Testimony by John Denson apologizing for having been a witness to Thomas Sikes marriage.

Consent given to Joseph Woodson to marry Mary Sandboarn by her father, Daniel Sandboarn, 9/11/1706.

Testimony by John Scot apologizing for wrongfully marrying one outside of the Quakers, 10/8/1707.

John Evans, Sr. disowned for drunkenness and fighting, 9/11/1706.

William Pope of Nansemond County promises to fulfill business pledge,

8/2/1708.

Daniel Akehust died 8/11/1699.

Richard Rickeses died 10 a.m. 20/7/1708.

Elizabeth Small of Nansemond County died 25/7/1717; Father: Edmund Belson Mother: Mary Belson.

Catherine Ricks died 1/8/1717.

William Scotte died 11/8/1717.

Isaac Ricks died 3/11/1723.

Richard Jordan died 29/10/1723.

Katheren Wiggs died 12/11/1678.

The burial of Jeams Hill: Rachill Hill buried 10/1/1674, Josife Hill buried 14/2/1674, Elizabeth Hill (wife of Jeams Hill), buried 16/3/1674, An Hill buried 16/8/1674.?

Hannah Outland, wife of Cornelius Outland, 11/1/1676.

Children of William Denson and Francis his wife: Francis, b. 1/12/1751; William, b. 25/11/1653; James, b. 11/8/1657; Katheren, b. 4/8/1659; Sarah, 14/11/1665; John b. 25/3/1666; Joseph, 18/8/1669.

William Denson died 8/1/1676.

Marriage of Cornelius Outland and Hannah Copeland, 5/3/1675, at Chuckatuck.

Cornelius Outland died 13/12/1676.

Children of William Page and Marie his wife: William, 15/8/1662; Henry, b. last of the eleventh month 1663; Alise, b. ?/8/1667; John, b. 6/8/1670.

Children of John Kensy of Carolina and Catherine his wife: John, b. 6/10/1692.

William Galliway died 27/5/1677.

Mary Copland, wife of Joseph Copland, died 27/3/1678.

William Yarrat died latter part of 1676.

Margaret Yarrat, wife of William Yarrat, the elder, died 1677.

Edmond Bellson died 19/1/1679.

Ruth Harris, daughter of John Harris, 11/4/1679.

William Yarrat, the elder, died 24/5/1687.

William Outeland died 24/5/1687.

Thomas Hollowell, the elder, died 16/1/1687.

Edmond Hollowell, son of Thomas Hollowell, died 10/2/1687.

Mary Belson, wife of Edmond Belson of Nansemond, 20/12/1687.

Christian Jordan, wife of Robart Jordan, 26/6/1689.

William Rickesis, son of Isaac Rickesis, died 22/6/1694 at about 24 years of age.

Alice Hollowell, widow of Thomas Hollowell 19/9/1700.

Jacob Rickesis, son of Isaac Rickesis and Kathren his wife, died ?/5/?
Children of Thomas Page and Isabell his wife: Thomas, b. 7/10/1703;
Elizabeth, b. 30/4/1706; Henry, 9/2/1708.
Children of Abraham Rickes and Mary his wife: Mary, b. 1/7/1704;
Elizabeth, b. 18/11/1706.
Children of Isaac Rickes, Jr. and Sarah his wife: William, b. 25/7/1698;
Isaac Rickes b. 27/12/1702; Jacob Rickes, 11/2/1705.
Certificate for Joseph Glaster; Daughter: Sarah Robinson.
Certificate for Nathan Nuby, 9/8/1707.
Levys taken from John Simons, 1704, 1706, 1707.
Certificate for Joseph Robinson, 21/8/1707.
Certificate for Peter Pearson, 23/7/1707.
Certificate for Thomas Glaister, 12/7/1707.
Certificate for Thomas Robinson, 17/7/1707.
Margarett Jordan b. seventh month, 1642; d. 17/10/1708 Father: Robert
Brashare.
Decision of mens meeting at Chuckatuck for the meeting in Perquimons,
NC, that Isaac Willson ought to make payment, given by Robert
Willson,(the testator) to Sarah Bellman or her heirs, 8/1/1703.
William Scot testifies against the sin of drunkenness, fifth month of 1705.
Priest dues taken from friends in Nansemond County: Margaret Jordan
100 pounds of tobacco, 25/1/1701; Robert Jordan all his levis for the
present year except ten pounds of tobacco, 25/10/1700; Margaret
Jordan, Sr. one hogshead of tobacco, Feb. 18, 1701.
Thomas Jordan imprisoned 6 weeks for being taken at a meeting at his
house and bound over to Nansemond County Court for being taken at
a meeting at Robert Lawrence's house, imprisoned at Jamestown for
ten months for refusing to swear in court, three servants taken and
kept nine weeks, also taken furniture and other goods and a servant
man that had three years to serve and cattle in Chuckatuck, first day
of the seventh month, 1661.
Priests dues taken: James Jordan 357 pounds of tobacco, April 2, 1703;
Richard Rattcliff 1795 pounds of tobacco, January 20, 1703; Richard
Rattcliff, Sr. 160 pounds of tobacco in Isle of Wight County, 1703;
Richard Rattcliff, 179 pounds of tobacco, Feb. 24, 1704.
Marriage of Richard Jordan of Chuckatuck and Rebecca Rattcliff of
Trernasco Necks, 22 day of the sixth month, 1706; Fathers: Thomas
Jordan (deceased) and Richard Ratclif; Brother: Benjamin Jordan,
Jonathan Jordan, Robert Jordan, Joshua Jordan, James Jordan,
Richard Rattclif, Jonathan Rattcliff; Mothers: Elizabeth Rattcliff,
Margaret Jordan.

Marriage of William Pope and Mary Haile of Nansemond County, 11 day of 2nd month, 1708.

Marriage of William Scott and Christian Jordan of Nansemond County, 28th day, sixth month, 1707; Fathers: John Scott, Robert Jordan; Mother: Elis Small; Grandmother: Margaret Jordan

Marriage of James Denson and Sarah Dryton of Isle of Wight County, 15 day, 11 month, 1707; Mother: Frances Denson.

Marriage of William Denson of Isle of Wight County and Amey Small of Nansemond County, 20/12/1723. Fathers: John Denson, Benjamin Small.

William Scott testifies to having been drunk, 5/3/1703.

Meeting house built on land bought from Frances Hutchins, paid for by members of the meeting: Francis Bridle; Isaac Rickes, Sr.; William Scott, Sr.; James Denson; Jonathan Denson; Abraham Rickes; Jonathan Rickes; Robert Rickes; Jonathan Sikes; Thomas Hampton; Francis Denson.

Minutes of Pagan Creek 1738 - 1763

7/7/1738. William Outland and Mary Ratlyff to marry.

2/9/1738. Joseph Pretlow and Sara Scott to marry.

7/10/1738. James Took Scott and Christian Narsworthy to marry.

1/1/1738/9. Jacob Powell and Sarah Bullock to marry.

1/1/1738/9. Pleasants Jordan and Mary Corbin to marry.

2/6/1739. Thomas Draper and Patianc Denson to marry.

6/7/1739. Richard Matthis and Rebeckah Pinner to marry.

4/7/1740. Joseph Hollowell and Martha Williams to marry.

6/9/1740. John Lawrance and Martha Ricks to marry.

6/9/1740. John Pleasants and Elizabeth Scott to marry.

6/9/1740. John Pinnear and Sarah Scott to marry.

2/2/1741. John Outland and Elizabeth Wilkinson to marry.

6/6/1741. Jacob Johnson and Mary Denson to marry.

3/10/1741. Samual Hargrove and Sarah Pretlow to marry.

7/11/1741. William Outland and Rachel White to marry.

1/5/1742. William Wiggs and Lidia Sebrell to marry.

4/9/1742. William Scott and Elizabeth Ricks to marry.

7/2/1743. Frances Bracy and Ann Jordan to marry.

6/8/1743. Thomas Newby and Mary Pretlow to marry.

3/9/1743. John Porter and Betty Denson to marry.

5/1/1743/4. Joseph Denson and Christian Ealey to marry.

-/10/1744. Thomas Outland and Elizabeth White to marry.
-/10/1744. Thomas Pretlow and Mary Ricks to marry.
-/10/1744. Robart Johnson and Christian Outland to marry.
-/10/1744. James Copland and Martha Johnson to marry.
20/12/1745. Lewis Whithead and Mary Watkins to marry.
20/1/1746. Josiah Jordan and Morning Ricks to marry.
17/2/1746. Tryal Baley and Paticene Brasey to marry.
16/8//1746. Matthew Jordan and Mary Brasey to marry.
16/8/1746. Richard Pope and Ann Williams to marry.
19/1/1746/7. Daniel Sebrell and Margret Jordan to marry.
18/4/1747. William Denson and Ann Watkins to marry.
18/4/1747. Burns Clary and Mary Jordan to marry.
20/6/1747. Benjamin Denson and Mary Whithead to marry.
15/8/1747. Lazarus Johnson and Mary Outland to marry.
17/11/1747. John Outland and Elizabeth Brasy to marry.
19/11/1748. Jesse Hargrove and Naomey Sebrell to marry.
16/9/1749. Thomas Copeland and Mary Murrey to marry.
18/11/1749. Joseph Newby and Patience Jordan to marry.
15/12/1749. John Cheadles and Elizabeth Hargrave to marry.
15/12/1749. Joshua White and Mary Cornwell to marry.
15/1/1750. Absolum Hollowell and Mary Hargrave to marry.
21/1/1750/51. Moses Sebrell and Sarah Hargrave to marry.
17/2/1751. William Holowell and Sarah Cofield to marry.
18/5/1751. Richard Ricks and Ann Jarret to marry.
16/1/1752. Jesse Ladd and Margret Whitfield to marry.
16/4/1752. Holowel Denson and Martha Cofeild to marry.

Papers of Denial

Elizabeth Denson, disorderly marriage, 4/4/1743.
Elizabeth Sebrell, disorderly walking, 2/4/1743.
Morning Clany, disorderly marriage, 7/4/1743.
Elizabeth Matthis, disorderly marriage, 17/11/1744.
Ann Ricks, disorderly marriage, 23/9/1745.
Dorothy Jordan (widow of Matthew Jordan), disorderly walking, 19/2/1750.
Dorothy Davis, disorderly marriage, 24/4/1750.
Martha Simmons, dau. of John Simmons of Prince George Co., disorderly marriage, marrying her first cousin by a hireling priest, 20/3/1764.
Sarah Briggs, dau. of Nathaniel Briggs of Sussex Co., disorderly marriage, and against her parent's will. 15/1/1763.
Anne Hitchen, dau. of James Kitchen, dec'd., of Southampton Co.,

disorderly marriage, taking a husband by a hireling priest, 16/4/1763.

WESTERN BRANCH MONTHLY MEETING
Minutes 1767 - 1771

J. L. Outland, son of Richard Exum Outland of --- Co. is disowned, 24/5/1767.

Mourning Pope, dau. of Henry(?) Pope, late of --- Co. has taken a husband by a hireling priest disowned, 21/11/1766.

28/3/1767. Certificate for Thomas Outland and wife and children to monthly meeting at Rich Square, NC. Aron Barber and Mary Manning to marry. Certificate requested for Joseph Jones, son of William Jones, to Blackwater Monthly Meeting. Elizabeth Ricks, wife of Thomas Ricks, produced a certificate from the monthly meeting at Blackwater. Black Creek Meeting reports that Josiah Johnson has taken a wife by a hireling priest - disowned.

25/4/1767. James Lad and Isbell Denson to marry. Sufferings: James Jordan Scott - 1.11.8; Jacob Vicks - 3.6.0; Richard Vicks - 1.8.0; Benjamin Denson - 1.0.0; William Jones - 1.7.4. Mary Edmunds requests to be taken under the care of Friends.

23/5/1767. James Lad produced a certificate from his monthly meeting. Francis Brasey and Mary Edmunds to marry.

27/6/1767. Marriage of James Lad orderly accomplished. David Denson of Black Creek Meeting marriage by a hireling priest - disowned. Isbell, wife of James Ladd requests a certificate to monthly meeting at White Oak Swamp. Complaint is made by Thomas Newby as executor of John Trotter and by Melicent Murdaugh, also by Joseph Scott in behalf of Thomas Pleasants, Junr. that Thos. Trotter stands indebted to each of them for some time.

25/7/1767. Marriage of Francis Brasey orderly accomplished.

A list of names given to the Colonel of each county within the limits of our Monthly Meeting [*as pacifists*]:

Nansemond Co: Joseph Robinson, John Jordan, Senr., Robert Jordan, Joseph Scott, Robert Abrahams, William Robinson, Edward Everagin, Edmund Jordan, John Jordan, Junr., Christopher Jordan, Robert Jordan, Junr., Joseph Randolph, Thomas Trotter, Pleasant Jordan, Joseph Prichard, Edmund Outland, James Winbour, John Porter, James Copland of Henry, Jesse Johnson, Elisha Copland, John Copland, Silas Copland, John Copland of Jams., Junr., Thomas Draper, Junr., Benjamin Russell, ..dom Harrall, Thomas Harrell, James Harrell, Henry Hair.

Norfolk Co.: Joseph Jordan, Joseph Jordan, Junr.

Isle of Wight Co.: John Lawrance, John Lawrance, Junr., Samuel Lawrance, John Outland, Benjamin Whitfield, Matthew Jordan, Matthew Jordan, Junr., Jacob Powell, John Pritlow, Richard Jordan, John Jordan, Jessee Watkins, Robert Johnson, Lazaruss Johnson, Robert Johnson, Junr., Josiah Jordan, Hezeciah Jordan, Thomas Jordan, Elijah Johnson, Mordica Powell, Richard Parr, Wm. Parr, Antony Parr, John Marshall, Junr., John Denson.

Southampton Co.: William Jones, James Jordan Scott, Thomas Draper, Francis Brasey, Benjamin Denson, Thomas Ricks, Robert Ricks, Demsy Johnson, William Draper, Jesse Draper, Jessey Draper, Jeremiah Draper, Jethrough Denson, Jordan Denson, Laskie Denson, Jacob Vicks, John Cathon, Jacob Vicks, Junr., Jessey Vicks, William Scott.

26/9/1767. Sufferings: Benjamin Whitfield, Lazarus Johnson. Black Creek Meeting reports that Dorathy Denson has consented to marriage with a man not of our Society - disowned.

26/12/1767. Moses Harriss and Saphire Eley to marry.

23/1/1768. Joseph Butler and Ann Thomas to marry. Certificate for Sarah Parker, wife of Joseph Parker of Northampton Co., NC, to Rich Square Monthly Meeting. Robert Jordan, Junr., requests certificate to monthly meeting in Henrico Co. Robert Jordan, Senr. requests certificate for himself and family to monthly meeting in Northampton Co., NC. Informed that John Jordan has taken a wife by a hireling priest - disowned. Informed that Patience Jordan, the Younger, is about to join in marriage with a man not of our Society [disowned].

27/2/1768. Marriage of Moses Harriss orderly accomplished. Joseph Butler produced a certificate from his monthly meeting. Reported by Summaton Meeting that John Copland continues practice of drunkenness - disowned. Benjamin Russell requests to become a member [received]. Reported that Mourning Johnson has consented to marriage with a man not of our Society [disowned]. Saphire, wife of Moses Harriss requests certificate to monthly meeting at Seder [Cedar] Creek.

26/3/1768. Marriage of Joseph Butler accomplished.

23/4/1768. Summerton Meeting reports that Ann Harrwell has consented to marriage with a man not of our Society - disowned.

[... missing pages]

27/8/1768. James Butler and Persilla Thomas to marry. Silvah Hargrave requests to be received into membership. Reported that William Parr is about to take a wife contrary to Discipline [disowned]. Reported that Luke Denson has walked disorderly for some time. Thomas

Draper in behalf of Matthew Jones, late administrator of Joseph Denson, requested approval to bring suit against Benjamin Denson for recovery of some tobacco which was recovered by Benjamin Denson from said Denson's estate which said Jones since has found to be illegal - approved.

24/9/1768. Demsy (Dempsey) Watts disowned. John Lawrence, Junr. request certificate signifying his clearness in marriage, to monthly meeting of Rich Square, NC. Reported that James Harrell son of John, has taken a wife contrary to Discipline [disowned].

26/11/1768. [Sickness of Pricilla Thomas has delayed her marriage.] Robert Johnson the younger and Sylvia Hargrave to marry.

28/1/1769. Marriage of Robert Johnson, Junr. accomplished. Reported that Hezekiah Jordan has joined in marriage with his cousin by a priest - disowned.

25/2/1769. Zachariah Copeland and Sarah Poter to marry. Henry Hair and Jean Johnston to marry. Matthew Jones and Ann Lawrence to marry, he to produce a certificate from his monthly meeting. Certificate for Jesse Vick signifying his clearness in marriage to Rich Square Monthly Meeting, NC.

[... missing minutes for 3 and 4th month 1769...]

27/5/1769. Marriage of Zachariah Copland accomplished. Certificate requested for John Lawrence, Junr. to monthly meeting at Rich Square, NC.

24/6/1769. Receiving letter from Rich Square Monthly Meeting stating that James Copland of James regarding his disorderly walking, he is disowned. Certificate requested for Matthew Jones to monthly meeting at Blackwater. Robert Saunder and Stephen Langford request to be received into membership - received.

26/8/1769. Informed that Jethrough Denson has taken a wife by a Justice of the Peace - disowned.

[...missing about 10 sets of minutes...]

25/8/1770. Aron Barber disowned. William Scott and Elizabeth Trotter to marry. Ann Balmer received into membership.

22/9/1770. Armijar Bailey and Ann Balmer to marry. Reported that James Denson, son of Francis, has behaved disorderly [disowned].

27/11/1770. James Bacon(?) disowned. Marriage of William Scott accomplished. Edmund Jordan and Sarah Draper to marry.

24/11/1770. Marriage of Armiger Bailey accomplished. Sarah Harrell, dau. of John Harrell, condemns his past conduct and requests to be taken under the notice of Friends. Blackwater Monthly Meeting states that Matthew Kitchin under necessity of some relief and asks if he is still a member of this monthly meeting.

22/12/1770. Marriage of Edmund Jordan accomplished. Elijah Johnson and Mary Winburn to marry.

Marriage of Joseph Butler, son of James Butler of Dinwiddie Co., and Ann Thomas, dau. of John Thomas of Nansemond Co., with consent of parents ... [rest of page missing...]

26/1/1771. Complaint of disorderly walking of John Outland [disowned].

[missing about 7 minutes ...]

28/9/1771. Jordan Clary and Hannah Jordan to marry.

26/10/1771. Jordan Clary since last meeting has died. Hanour Beal wishes to become a member.

23/11/1771. Charles Clary and Elizabeth Jordan to marry. Sarah Eley requests to become a member [received].

28/12/1771. Lamuell Jones and Cathern Lawrance to marry.

-A-
ABRAHAMS, Robert, 52
AKEHUST, Daniel, 48
ANDREWS, Elizabeth, 1; Jane,
1; John, 1, 21, 22, 25, 39;
Joseph, 1; Martha, 1; Robert,
1; Sarah, 1
ANTHONY, Christopher, 18
ATKINSON, Ann, 12; Median,
24; Medion, 22; Robert, 13,
19, 20, 28

-B-
BACON, James, 54
BAIELY, Judith, 2
BAILEY, Abadan, 4; Abidan, 2,
3, 16, 34; Abiden, 16; Abidon,
28; Abigail, 2; Abigal, 4;
Absalom, 11, 12, 25; Absolam,
28; Absolom, 20; Ann, 1, 2, 3,
4, 23, 32, 37, 39; Anselm, 11,
12, 13, 16, 19, 37, 38;
Armiger, 33; Armijar, 54;
Barak, 4; Benjamin, 2, 8, 13,
16, 19, 20, 24, 25, 30, 38;
Bethany, 3; Daniel, 2; David,
2; Delitha, 2, 34; Demy, 21;
Denny, 21; Ebeden, 12;
Ebiden, 16; Edmon, 3, 31;
Edmond, 1, 2, 34, 36, 38;
Edmund, 4, 12; Edna, 3;
Edward, 24; Elijah, 1, 3, 4, 11,
12, 13, 19, 28; Elizabeth, 1, 2,
3, 4, 16, 36; Exam, 2; Exum,
34; Faith, 1, 8, 31; Henry, 4;
James, 1, 2, 33, 36; Jane, 3,
29, 33; Jesse, 1, 2, 4, 31; Joel,
23; John, 2, 15, 16, 19, 30, 33;
Joseph, 2, 4, 11, 12, 13, 24,
28; Joseph G., 19; Joseph

Glaister, 24; Joshua, 2, 3, 12,
18; Josiah, 2; Lazerus, 2;
Lemuel, 18, 22, 27, 29; Lucy,
1, 2, 3, 19; Margaret, 8;
Mariah, 3; Martha, 2, 23, 34,
38; Mary, 2, 11, 16, 18, 28,
35, 37; Mathew, 1, 2, 35;
Micajah, 1, 2, 11, 36; Michael,
13, 15, 25, 28, 29, 33; Michal,
2, 4; Miriam, 2, 11; Mourning,
4, 23; Patience, 1, 2, 3, 31;
Peninah, 2; Penninah, 37;
Permelia, 4; Peterson, 2;
Pharaba, 4; Pheruba, 31;
Priscilla, 4; Rachel, 2;
Rebecah, 3, 4; Rebecca, 2, 3,
30; Rebeckah, 2, 3, 4; Robert,
25, 30; Ruth, 32, 37; Sam, 16;
Samuel, 1, 2, 4, 8, 14, 31, 32,
34, 35, 38, 39; Sarah, 1, 2, 19,
21, 32, 38, 39; Stephen, 1, 2;
Susanna, 2; Tryal, 11, 18;
Tryall, 23; Uriah, 4; Ursuly,
36; William, 1, 2, 3, 4, 24;
Wyatt, 3; Zachariah, 2, 35
BALEY, Tryal, 51
BALMER, Ann, 54
BARBER, Aron, 52, 54
BARKER, John, 14; Mary, 14, 15
BARNES, John, 45
BASNETT, Richard, 45
BATES, James, 37
BEAL, Hanour, 54
BELLMAN, Sarah, 49
BELLSON, Edmond, 46, 48;
Isaac, 46; Jacob, 46; John, 46;
Kathren, 46; Mary, 46;
Robert, 46
BELSON, Edmond, 42, 43, 45,
48; Elizabeth, 42, 43; Mary,

42, 43, 48
BENSON, Frances, 45; Francis,
45; John, 45; Sara, 45
BETTS, Banester, 34; Banister,
20; Bannester, 19
BILLINGSLY, George, 43
BINFORD, Agness, 4; Ann, 1;
Aquila, 3; Aquilla, 3, 4, 28;
Benjamin, 3; Chappel, 1, 21,
39; Elizabeth, 1, 3, 39; Equil-
la, 12; Gule Elma, 3; Guli, 3;
Guli Elma, 1; James, 1, 3, 4,
12, 17, 20, 21, 22, 27, 39;
Jane, 1; Jesse, 26; John, 4;
Jonathan, 3, 4; Lemuel, 1;
Martha, 1, 3, 4; Mary, 1, 3, 4,
11, 14, 21; Michal, 4; Peter, 1,
2, 3, 4, 13, 22, 23, 30, 37, 38,
39; Peter Cappell, 20; Priscil-
la, 31, 37; Rebeckah, 2, 3;
Robert, 1; Ruth, 17; Samuel,
1, 35, 36; Sarah, 3, 36, 37, 38;
Thomas, 12, 16, 17, 19, 20,
21, 22, 23, 26; William, 38
BOGUE, William, 47
BOTT, Elizabeth, 10, 39; Susan-
na, 10; Susannah, 14; William,
10, 14, 15, 26, 31, 39
BOTTOM, Mary, 30
BRACY, Frances, 50
BRAISE, Francis, 46; Hugh, 46
BRASEY, Francis, 52, 53; Mary,
51; Paticene, 51
BRASHARE, Robert, 49
BRASSER, Abagall, 44
BRASSERE, John, 44
BRASSERES, John, 44
BRASY, Eilzabeth, 51
BRESSIE, Hugh, 43; William, 43
BRIDDELL, Francis B., 47
BRIDELL, Francis, 45; Mary, 45

BRIDLE, Francis, 50
BRIGGS, Ann, 24; Elizabeth, 34;
James, 30; Mary, 13; Nathan,
12; Nathaniel, 27, 51;
Priscilla, 15; Prissilla, 14;
Sarah, 51
BROCK, Abigail, 2; Burwell, 1, 3;
James, 1, 2, 3, 17, 38; Lucy,
11; Martha, 1, 30; Michal, 2;
Pharaby, 1; Pheraby, 33;
Rhoda, 2; Sara, 1; Sarah, 2, 3
BROSY, Susanna, 46; William, 47
BROWNE, John, 45
BUDD, Mahlon, 28, 29
BUFKIN, Dorrithy, 42, 45;
Leaven, 42
BULLOCK, Sarah, 50
BURGH, Elizabeth, 43; Margret,
44; Mourrning, 43; William,
43
BUTLAR, Elizabeth, 1; John, 1;
Lydia, 1; Mary, 2; Stephen, 2;
William, 2
BUTLER, Abidian, 3; Ann, 1, 2,
3, 8, 19, 20, 24, 25, 31; Cirly,
4; Daniel, 4, 25, 26, 34; David,
4; Edward, 1, 3, 31; Elisabeth,
39; Elizabeth, 1, 2, 25, 29, 30,
34; Henry, 3; Hulda, 1;
James, 1, 3, 4, 13, 14, 18, 19,
21, 22, 25, 26, 31, 33, 35, 38,
41, 53, 54; James Stanton, 2;
Jane, 25; Jas., 24; Jesse, 24;
John, 2, 4, 13, 18, 19, 20, 21,
24, 25, 26, 31, 34, 37, 41;
Jonathan, 1, 2, 3; Joseph, 1,
2, 3, 4, 8, 13, 14, 18, 19, 20,
24, 25, 26, 39, 53, 54; Josiah,
2; Lazaruz, 1; Lucy, 4; Lydia,
4, 35; Margrat, 1; Margret
Whitfield, 3; Martha, 1, 2, 3,

18, 19, 25, 31, 39; Mary, 1, 2, 3, 4, 11, 24, 25, 31, 32, 34, 35, 38; Micajah, 1; Miriam, 1, 3, 39; Mourning, 3, 4; Nancy, 1; Nathan, 4; Penniah, 24; Penninah, 1; Prisa, 25; Priscilla, 1, 3, 24, 31; Robert, 3, 4, 25, 31; Robert Hunnicutt, 1; Samuel, 1, 4, 27, 28, 29; Sarah, 1, 4, 25, 31, 39; Simon, 3; Stanton, 34; Steaphen, 18; Steph, 3; Stephen, 1, 2, 4, 19, 20, 21, 25, 34; Susanna, 8; Susannah, 12; Tabitha, 1, 4, 11, 31; Tillman, 1; Tilmon, 3, 25; Urlsy, 4; Wallace, 16; Wallis, 16; William, 1, 4, 13, 16, 18, 19, 20, 21, 35, 39, 41

BUTTLER, John, 37

-C-

CAMPION, Sara, 43

CARY, Sarah, 35

CATHON, John, 53

CHAPMAN, Benjamin, 47

CHAPPEL, Agnes, 17; Agness, 4, 16, 21; Benjamin, 4, 21; Benjmn., 13; Elizabeth, 4, 24; Jane, 34; John, 4; Mary, 4, 28; Thomas, 4, 31

CHAPPELL, Agness, 4, 22; Benjamin, 12, 25; Jane, 4; John, 5; Mariah, 4

CHEADLES, John, 51

CLANY, Morning, 51

CLAREY, James, 12

CLARY, Ann, 14; Barnet, 13; Burns, 51; Charles, 16, 30, 54; Elizabeth, 11; James, 38; Jordan, 14, 15, 54; Lucy, 32; Martha, 20; Mary, 35;

Thomas, 35

COFEILD, Martha, 51

COFIELD, Sarah, 51

COKER, Jonathan, 22

COLLINGS, John, 45

COOK, Betty, 4; Joel, 4; John, 4; Josiah, 4, 21, 30, 36; Lidia, 36; Lydia, 4; Mary, 36; Priscilla, 4; William, 36

COPELAND, Hannah, 48; Thomas, 51; Zachariah, 54

COPLAND, Elisha, 52; Henry, 52; James, 51, 52, 54; John, 52, 53; Joseph, 48; Mary, 47, 48; Silas, 52

CORBIN, Mary, 50

CORNWELL, Aaron, 23, 27; Ann, 18, 26, 27, 38; Aron, 14, 18; Arron, 13; Elizabeth, 12, 26, 27; Jacob, 20, 22, 23, 27; John, 12, 13, 26, 27, 29, 30, 39; Joseph, 23; Joseph Crew, 23; Mary, 12, 25, 51; Moses, 27; Mourning, 11, 26; Samuel, 21, 38, 39; William, 27, 29, 32

COTCHING, Elizabeth, 44; Thomas, 44

CREW, Anna, 33; Anne, 4; Caleb, 24, 33; Charles, 24, 33; Elizabeth, 33; Hannah, 33, 34; Hardy, 21; John, 4, 24, 33; John Ellison, 4; Joshua, 4, 24, 33; Judith, 4, 24, 33; Margaret, 12; Martha, 24, 33; Sarah, 31, 33; Sarah Ladd, 4

CREWE, Mary, 42

CREWS, Andrew, 38; Benjamin, 12, 38; Ellyson, 19

CROW, Hannah, 34

CRYER, Elisabeth, 11

-D-

DAVICE, Josiah, 35

DAVIS, Ann, 32; David, 12, 16,
28, 38; Dorothy, 51;
Elizabeth, 37; James, 44;
Margaret, 44; Rebecca, 29;
Thomas, 42

DAWSON, William, 46

DENSON, Benjamin, 51, 52, 53,
54; Betty, 50; David, 52;
Dorathy, 53; Elizabeth, 18,
51; Frances, 43, 50; Francis,
48, 50, 54; Holowel, 51; Isbell,
52; James, 43, 48, 50, 54;
Jethrough, 53, 54; John, 47,
48, 50, 53; Jonathan, 50;
Jordan, 53; Joseph, 20, 48,
50, 54; Kateren, 48; Laskie,
53; Luke, 53; Mary, 50;
Patianc, 50; Sarah, 43, 48;
Thomas, 11; William, 18, 48,
50, 51

DILWORTH, Ann, 35

DRAPER, Jeremiah, 53; Jesse,
53; Jessey, 53; Matthew, 54;
Sarah, 54; Thomas, 50, 52, 53,
54; William, 53

DRYTON, Sarah, 50

DUKE, Margrett, 47; Mary, 46;
Sarah, 47; Thomas, 14, 44, 46,
47

DUPREE, Lewis, 24

DUPRESS, Lewis, 22

DURHAM, Esther, 31

DURPICE, Lewis, 24

-E-

EALEY, Christian, 50

EDMUNDS, Mary, 52

EL..Y, Agathy, 37; Caster, 37;
Kezier, 37

ELAMS, Emannuel, 12; Samuel,
12

ELEY, Saphire, 53; Sarah, 54

ELLIS, Edward, 24; Edwin, 20,
22, 24

ELLISON, Sarah, 37

ELLYSON, Darcus, 24; Elijah,
24; Gerrot Robert, 24

ELLZEY, William, 26

ELY, Lemuel, 34

EVANS, Jane, 32, 34, 39; John,
47; Robert, 34, 39

EVENS, Robert, 17

EVERAGIN, Edward, 52

EXUM, Jeremiah, 46; Mary, 46

-F-

FISHER, David, 17, 18, 20, 22,
28, 39

FOAKE, Mary, 45

FOOK, Joan, 47; Thomas, 47

FOWLER, Eliz., 12; Elizabeth, 5;
Godfree, 38; Henry, 13; John,
12, 13, 15, 16, 19, 20, 23, 25,
38; Martha, 5, 22; Mary, 5,
19, 20, 21; Paul, 5; Simmons,
5, 12; William, 26

FULLER, Sara, 45

-G-

GALLIWAY, William, 48

GARRETT, Cathren, 42;
Katheren, 42; Mary, 42

GAY, Jonathan, 12, 17; Thomas,
46

GLAISTER, Thomas, 49

GLASTER, Joseph, 49

GORDEN, Ann C., 31

-H-

HACKLET, Henry, 47

Thomas, 43, 44, 45, 48;
William, 6, 34, 36
HOLOWELL, William, 51
HORN, Thomas, 26
HORSEFALL, Mary, 33, 34
HORSFALL, Edmond, 33; Mary,
33
HOUSE, Mary, 18, 38
HOWARD, Sara, 44
HOWERD, Phil, 44
HUNNICTT, Peter, 38; William,
38
HUNNICUT, Wyke, 12, 37
HUNNICUTT, Ann, 5, 6, 15, 19,
29, 39; Anna, 5; Anselm, 5;
Benjamin, 22; Daniel, 5;
Deborah, 6; Delitha, 6;
Edward, 5; Elisabeth, 18;
Elizabeth, 5, 6, 36, 37;
Ephraim, 5; Glaister, 5, 12,
14, 21, 25, 26, 39; Hannah,
34; James, 5, 6, 12, 16, 34, 38;
Jane, 5, 22, 27, 28, 31; Jess,
32; Jesse, 5, 12, 30, 32; John,
5, 11, 12, 13, 20, 21, 22, 37,
38, 40; John Pearson, 6;
Joshua Bailey, 6; Lemuel, 5;
Margreat, 15; Margret, 38;
Marian, 6; Mark, 5; Martha,
5, 6, 39; Mary, 5, 6, 17, 27,
30, 35, 39; Meriam, 6, 14, 15,
38; Miriam, 5, 6; Peter, 5, 6,
12, 17, 38, 39; Pleasant, 5;
Pleasants, 21, 22; Precila, 35;
Priscilla, 38; Prisillah, 35;
Prissilla, 15; Robert, 5, 6, 11,
12, 13, 15, 16, 17, 19, 20, 21,
25, 34, 37, 38, 39; Robert
Wyke, 37, 38; Ruth, 5, 11;
Samuel, 5, 33; Sarah, 5, 14,
16, 20, 24, 35, 38, 39, 40;

Susanna, 5; Tabitha, 5;
Thomas, 6, 12, 17, 18, 20, 31,
36, 40; Thomas Pleasant, 5;
William, 5, 6, 12, 13, 14, 16,
17, 19, 20, 21, 24, 27, 30, 35,
38, 40; Wyke, 13, 14, 15, 19,
20, 21, 27, 38, 41; Wyle, 12,
13; Wythe, 5, 6
HUTCHINS, Frances, 50

-I-
INMAN, Hannah, 11

-J-
JARAD, Nicholas, 27
JARRAD, Nicholas, 28
JARRET, Ann, 51
JARROT, Nicholas, 21
JARROTT, Nicholas, 22
JOHNSON, Benjamin, 18, 35,
39; David, 39; Demsy, 53;
Elijah, 53, 54; Elisha, 29;
Elizabeth, 30, 35; Jacob, 50;
Jesse, 52; Josiah, 52; Lazarus,
27, 51, 53; Lazaruss, 53;
Lemuel, 36; Martha, 51;
Mary, 28, 39; Mourning, 53;
Nancy, 35; Rebecca, 35;
Robart, 51; Robert, 53, 54
JOHNSTON, Elizabeth, 36;
Jean, 54; Mary, 37
JONES, James, 7, 29, 30;
Joseph, 13, 52; Jucy, 29;
Lamuell, 54; Matthew, 12, 13,
14, 54; Robart, 45; William,
52, 53
JORDAN, Abigail, 42; Abigal, 45;
Ann, 45, 50; Ann Lutisha, 7;
Anne, 42; Bellsen, 45;
Benjamin, 42, 49; Christian,
44, 48, 50; Christopher, 52;

MATTHIS, Richard, 50
MERIMOON, Elizabeth, 7;
    Hannah, 7; Obedianic, 7;
    Peter, 7; Rhoda, 7; Robert, 7
MERIOTT, Mourning, 11;
    William, 25
MERRIDETH, Joseph, 45; Sam-
    son, 45
MERRIMON, Margaret, 14;
    Obediance, 14
MERRIOT, Benjamin, 11
MERRIOTT, John, 25; William,
    25
MERRYMOON, David, 15, 38;
    Davis, 13; Francis, 13, 14;
    Hannah, 13, 14, 38; John, 13,
    14, 38; Margaret, 13, 38;
    Peter, 13, 14
MOORE, Joshua, 37
MORRY, John, 43
MURDAUGH, Melicent, 52
MURDOCK, Priscilla, 31
MURDOUGH, John, 11
MURRELL, Elizabeth, 46;
    George, 46
MURREY, John, 45; Mary, 51

-N-
NARSWORTHY, Christian, 50
NEGRO, Abraham, 41; Aggey,
    40, 41; Amy, 41; Annaky, 41;
    Beck, 40; Ben, 21, 41; Bett,
    41; Bob, 40; Cate, 40; Char-
    les, 21; Charlet, 21; Cuffey,
    39; Cupid, 40; Davie, 40; Dick,
    40, 41; Dol, 41; Duke, 41;
    Fillis, 41; Fortune, 40;
    Gaberal, 41; Grace, 40; Han-
    nah, 41; James, 41; Janny, 41;
    Jemmy, 40, 41; Jenny, 21, 41;
    Jesse, 41; Jim, 40; Jimmy, 41;

Joan, 40; Joe, 21, 40; Judy,
    41; Kinchin, 40; Lewis, 40;
    Linn, 41; Lucy, 40; Lyddy, 40;
    Milly, 40, 41; Moses, 40, 41;
    Nanny, 40; Nathan, 40; Ned,
    40; Nedd, 41; Peter, 40, 41;
    Phebe, 40; Roger, 40; Sam,
    40, 41; Siar, 40; Silla, 41;
    Tom, 21, 40; Toney, 41; Will,
    41
NEUELL, John, 42
NEWBY, Ann, 32; Dorrithy, 42;
    Joseph, 32, 51; Thomas, 13,
    14, 15, 17, 50, 52; William, 42
NEWMAN, Thomas, 45
NICHOLSON, Mary, 25
NIXON, Barnaby, 7, 20, 21;
    David, 7; Perce, 29; Samuel,
    7; Sarah, 7, 26; Thomas, 29
NUBY, Nathan, 49
NUDBY, Thomas, 12

-O-
OADELANTS, William, 47
OGBURN, Pheaby, 13; Pheba,
    13
OUDELAND, Christian, 44
OUDELANT, Christian, 43, 44;
    Cornelius, 43; Thomas, 43;
    William, 43
OUDELANTS, Elizabeth, 43
OULDFEILD, Christopher, 44
OUTELAND, William, 48
OUTLAND, Christian, 51; Cor-
    nelius, 48; Edmund, 52; Han-
    nah, 48; J. L., 52; John, 50,
    51, 53, 54; Mary, 51; Richard
    Exum, 52; Thomas, 51, 52;
    William, 11, 50
OWEN, Ann, 47; Gilbert, 47

-P-

PAGE, Alce, 42; Alice, 46; Alise,
48; Elizabeth, 49; Henry, 48,
49; Isabell, 49; John, 47, 48;
Marie, 48; Mary, 46; Rebecca,
46; Rebecka, 42; Thomas, 42,
46, 49; William, 48
PARKER, Joseph, 53; Sarah, 53
PARR, Anthony, 53; Richard, 53;
William, 53
PARROTT, John, 44
PATTERSON, Benjamin, 31;
Jeremiah, 31; Joseph, 37;
Mary, 37
PATTISON, Benjamin, 13, 38;
Elisabeth, 13, 14; Elizabeth,
38; Hannah, 14; John, 15;
Kesiah, 14; Margaret, 14;
William, 14
PEARSON, Peter, 49
PEEBLES, Agness, 12; Anna, 7;
Butler, 7; Deborah, 8; Elijah,
8; Elisabeth, 15; Elisha, 8;
Elizabeth, 7, 8, 36; Huldah, 7;
Huldah Ladd, 8; James, 7, 8,
19, 20, 21; John, 8, 12, 21;
Josiah, 7; Lucy, 8; Margret, 8;
Mary, 8, 38; Micajah, 8; Mor-
decai, 7; Mourning, 7, 15, 26;
Penninah, 8; Peter, 7, 8, 12,
15, 16, 20, 21, 37; Samuel, 8;
Sarah, 7, 8, 37; Silviah, 7;
Stephen, 8, 24, 25, 29, 36;
Susanah, 25; Susanna, 7, 8,
34, 39; William, 7, 12, 20, 21;
William Ladd, 7; William
Scott, 8
PERKINS, Edward, 44
PERROTT, John, 45
PHILLIPS, Benjamina, 7;
George, 7; Henry, 7; James,

7; Samuel, 7
PINNEAR, John, 50
PINNER, John, 36; Rebeckah,
50; Sarah, 18
PLEASANTS, John, 15, 38, 50;
Meriam, 15; Thomas, 52
POPE, Henry, 52; Mourning, 52;
Richard, 51; William, 47, 50
PORTER, John, 50, 52
POTER, Sarah, 54
POWEL, Elizabeth, 46; Rebeca,
47; William, 46, 47
POWELL, Jacob, 50, 53; Mor-
dica, 53
PRETLOW, Ann, 11, 15, 22, 27;
Jane, 31; John, 12, 27;
Joseph, 50; Joshua, 15, 19,
38, 39; Mary, 27, 32, 39, 50;
Rebecca, 39; Rebeckah, 18,
38; Rebekah, 15, 16; Samuel,
13, 19, 23, 39; Sarah, 50;
Thomas, 12, 13, 14, 15, 19,
23, 39, 51
PRICHARD, Joseph, 52
PRITLOW, Anne, 8; Anselm, 8;
Benjamin, 34; John, 8, 53;
Joseph, 8; Joshua, 8; Mary
Anne, 8; Robert, 8; Samuel, 8,
11; Sarah, 8; Thomas, 8

-R-

RANDOLF, Joseph, 52
RATCLIF, Richard, 49
RATCLIFF, Cornelius, 46
RATLIFF, Cornelius, 46;
Elizabeth, 42, 46; John, 46;
Mary, 45, 46; Rebecca, 46;
Richard, 42, 45, 46; Sara, 45;
Sarah, 46
RATLYFF, Mary, 50
RATTCLIF, Jonathan, 49;

Richard, 49
RATTCLIFF, Elizabeth, 49;
    Rebecca, 49; Richard, 46, 49
RATTCLIFT, Elizabeth, 46;
    Rebecca, 46; Richard, 47
RATTLIFF, John, 47
REAMS, Hezekiah, 14, 17;
    Jeremiah, 14, 15; Jerimiah,
    38; William, 14, 15, 38
RICE, Martha, 45
RICHARDSON, John, 47
RICKES, Abraham, 49, 50; Isaac,
    46, 49, 50; Jacob, 46, 49;
    Jonathan, 50; Mary, 46, 49;
    Robart, 46; Robert, 29, 50;
    Sarah, 49; William, 49
RICKESES, Isaac, 49; Jacob, 49;
    Kathren, 49; Richard, 48
RICKESIS, Abraham, 43, 46;
    Benjamin, 43; Isaac, 43, 46,
    48; Jacob, 43, 46; James, 43;
    Jeane, 43; John, 43; Kathren,
    43; Richard, 43; Robert, 43;
    William, 43, 48
RICKS, Ann, 51; Catherine, 48;
    Elisabeth, 12; Elizabeth, 50,
    52; Isaac, 48; Martha, 50;
    Mary, 51; Morning, 51;
    Richard, 51; Robert, 22, 31,
    53; Samuel, 28, 29; Thomas,
    12, 52, 53
RIDICK, Joan, 45; Robart, 45
RIX, Abraham, 47; Mary, 47
ROBINSON, Joseph, 49, 52;
    Sarah, 49; Thomas, 49; Wil-
    liam, 52
ROSETER, Jane, 46
ROWE, Martha, 34
RUSSEL, Benjamin, 8, 9, 16, 17;
    Benjamin Bailey, 8; Lemuel,
    8; Mourning, 8, 9; Phebe, 8;

Rebecca, 8; Sophia, 8
RUSSELL, Benjamin, 29, 30, 52,
    53; Rebecah, 30; Sophia, 30
RUSSIL, Benjamin, 15

-S-

SADLER, Bartley, 9; Benjamin,
    9; Charles, 9; Elizabeth, 30;
    Fanny, 30; Henry, 25, 30;
    James, 30; Lucy, 9; Martha,
    9; Mary, 30; Nathaniel, 9;
    Rhoda, 9; Sarah, 9, 30, 35;
    Thomas, 9, 17, 22; William
    Rose, 9; Zachariah, 30
SANBOURN, Daniel, 47
SANDBOARN, Daniel, 47; Mary,
    47
SANDERS, William, 44
SAUNDER, Robert, 54
SCARS, John, 13
SCOT, John, 47; Sarah, 43; Wil-
    liam, 46, 47, 49
SCOTT, Ann, 11; Christian, 45;
    Elizabeth, 43, 50; George, 12,
    16; James Jordan, 52, 53;
    James Took, 50; John, 42, 43,
    50; Joseph, 52; Kathren, 43;
    Mary, 45; Robert, 18; Sara,
    50; Sarah, 50; Thomas, 12;
    William, 42, 43, 45, 50, 53, 54
SCOTTE, William, 48
SEARS, Ann, 30; Anna, 9;
    Elizabeth, 9, 38; Huldah, 9;
    Jemima, 29; John, 9, 13, 37;
    Martha, 9; Mary, 12; Meriam,
    9; Paul, 9, 32, 37, 38; Peter,
    9; Samuel, 9; Sarah, 9, 16, 26;
    Tabitha, 31
SEBRAL, Sarah, 11
SEBREL, Benjamin, 9, 36;
    Joseph, 9, 36; Josiah, 36;

-V-
VICK, Jesse, 54
VICKS, Jacob, 52, 53; Jessey, 53;
    Richard, 52

-W-
WALKER, John, 16
WALTHAL, Thomas, 29
WALTHALL, Elizabeth, 10;
    Francis, 10; Jane, 10; Susan-
    na, 10; Susannah, 10;
    Thomas, 10, 25, 39; William
    Bott, 10
WARD, John, 10; Kizia, 10;
    Mary, 10; Obed, 10; Ruth, 10;
    Stephen, 10; Susanna, 10;
    Timothy, 10, 15, 16, 25
WARREN, Elizabeth, 10, 23;
    Hannah, 10; John, 10; Peggy,
    35; Samuel, 10, 11, 13; Sarah,
    10
WARRIN, John, 29
WATERS, Mary, 46; Walter, 46
WATKINS, Ann, 10, 51; Ben-
    jamin, 10; James, 10, 13, 39,
    40; Jane, 18; Jessee, 53;
    John, 10, 11, 18; Joseph, 14;
    Mary, 10, 31, 51; Reubin, 10;
    Sarah, 10, 34; Susanna, 10;
    Winney, 10
WATTS, Dempsey, 54; Demsy,
    54
WEST, Anne, 11
WHITE, Ann, 10, 11, 39; Ben-
    jamin, 11; Clotilda, 11; Dazae,
    11; Dozae, 11; Elizabeth, 10,
    51; Francis, 27; Hannah, 17;
    John, 10, 11, 18, 26, 27, 32,
    38, 40, 46; Joshua, 51;
    Lemuel, 10, 32, 36; Lucy, 10;
    Mary, 10, 27, 35; Phranky,

10; Rachel, 50; Thomas, 46
WHITFIELD, Benjamin, 53;
    Margret, 51
WHITHEAD, Lewis, 51; Mary,
    51
WIGGS, Elizabeth, 42; Francis,
    46; Henry, 42, 46; Kateren,
    48; Sara, 42; William, 42, 50
WILKERSON, Sarah, 22, 23
WILKINSON, Elizabeth, 50;
    Henry, 47; William, 47
WILLIAMS, Ann, 51; James, 23;
    Martha, 50
WILLSON, Isaac, 49; Robert, 49
WINBOUR, James, 52
WINBURN, Mary, 54
WOMBLE, Eliza, 38
WOOD, Elizabeth, 44; John, 44;
    Margrett, 44
WOODSON, Joseph, 47
WREN, Alphred, 10; Anne, 10;
    Deborah, 10; Elijah, 10;
    Elitha, 10; Elizabeth, 10;
    Evans, 10, 25; Fanny, 10;
    Hannah, 10, 25; Julia, 10;
    Lucy, 10, 25; Lydia, 10; Mary,
    10; Richard, 10, 25; Sally, 10;
    Sucky, 10; William, 10, 25, 29
WRENN, Looky, 33; Lukey, 33;
    Lydia, 31; Richard, 21, 26, 33;
    Salley, 33; William, 31

-Y-
YARRAT, Margaret, 48
YARRETT, Elizabeth, 43, 44;
    Katheren, 44; Margrett, 44;
    William, 43, 44

www.ingramcontent.com/pod-product-compliance
Lightning Source LLC
Chambersburg PA
CBHW072212270326
41930CB00011B/2620